Anonymous

The New Testament of our Lord and Saviour Jesus Christ

Anonymous

The New Testament of our Lord and Saviour Jesus Christ

ISBN/EAN: 9783337146566

Printed in Europe, USA, Canada, Australia, Japan

Cover: Foto ©ninafisch / pixelio.de

More available books at **www.hansebooks.com**

THE TRIPLE COMPARISON

THE

NEW TESTAMENT

OF

OUR LORD AND SAVIOUR

JESUS CHRIST

TRANSLATED OUT OF THE GREEK

THE KING JAMES VERSION
  Of 1611, known as the Authorized Version;

THE ANGLICAN REVISED VERSION
  Of 1881, with Marginal Notes at the Foot;

THE AMERICAN REVISED VERSION
  Of 1881, having the Readings and Renderings preferred by the American Revisers embodied in the Text, by Rev. ROSWELL D. HITCHCOCK, D.D.

THE GOSPEL OF MARK

ARRANGED FOR USE IN SCHOOLS AND CLASSES

CONTAINING ALSO

LIST OF THE LESSONS FOR 1882, WITH GOLDEN TEXTS AND PAGE REFERENCES, and

CHRONOLOGICAL INDEX OF EVENTS IN THE LIFE OF CHRIST, WITH PAGE REFERENCES TO THOSE MENTIONED IN MARK'S GOSPEL

NEW YORK:
FORDS, HOWARD, & HULBERT
1882

PREFACE.

So many Sunday-school workers have shown special interest in the "American Version" of the revised New Testament, edited by Dr. Roswell D. Hitchcock, that, in response to frequent requests, a cheap "comparative edition" of the Gospel of Mark is herewith presented for Sunday-school use. This contains on one page, in clear, legible type, the King James version and the English revision with its marginal notes as foot-notes (following the style of the Oxford brevier edition), and on the opposite page the American Revised Version in full and fair long-primer type—so that all three versions may be readily compared. The American Version has been commended as "representing the best, the oldest, and the purest Greek text of the New Testament at present attainable, . . . and the most accurate English reading in existence of that Greek text." Dr. Hitchcock's admirable Preface to the American Version is given on the following pages, as a concise review of the whole question of Revision and the relative merits of the three representative English texts.

In addition to these three versions, thus presented side by side, the little pamphlet contains a full list of the Sunday-school Lessons for the entire year, with the Golden Texts and page-references, and a Chronological Index of events in the life of Christ, with special page-references to those mentioned by the evangelist Mark. It has been thought best not to encumber the work with any greater multiplication of references, comments, or other "helps."

THE PUBLISHERS.

NEW YORK, Dec., 1881.

CONTENTS.

	PAGE
PREFACE,	iii
PREFACE TO AMERICAN VERSION,	v
THE THREE VERSIONS (PAGES 62–100, FROM THE "TRIPLE COMPARATIVE EDITION,")	8–85
CHRONOLOGICAL INDEX OF EVENTS IN THE LIFE OF CHRIST, WITH PAGE REFERENCES TO THIS EDITION OF MARK,	87–89
THE LESSONS FOR 1882, WITH GOLDEN TEXTS, etc.,	91–96

PREFACE
TO THE
AMERICAN VERSION.

THE Canterbury Revision of the Authorized Version of the New Testament, which was begun in 1870 and finished in 1881, is an Anglo-American compromise. Had there been an Anglican Revision without American co-operation, the changes would have been fewer. Had there been an American Revision without Anglican co-operation, the changes would have been more numerous, and also more radical.

For nearly eleven years, the Anglican Company of twenty-five Revisers and the American Company of thirteen worked together, though more than three thousand miles apart. Most of the changes proposed by either Company were concurred in by the other Company. And yet, after all their mutual concessions, each side yielding more than it cared to yield, there remained a considerable number of rejected American suggestions, a list of which, partly in classes and partly in detail, is appended to the volume issued from the University Presses of Oxford and Cambridge.

These suggestions, which relate both to readings and to renderings, are here in this volume incorporated into the text. The present Editor, who was not one of the Revisers, considered it no part of his allotted task to make any other important changes than the ones thus indicated. He has merely worked up the suggestions of the Appendix; with the exception of adding one to the list of discarded archaisms by substituting "while" for "whiles," which occurs but twice.

It is proper to say, that neither the American Company of Revisers, nor any member of the Company, is responsible for the putting forth of this American Revision. The idea of it originated with the Publishers, whose names are on the title-page, and who have spared neither pains nor cost to have the work accurately done.

No book was ever translated perfectly; every language having its own characteristic idioms, for which there are no exact equivalents in other languages. But, on the whole, no book has endured translation better than the Bible. And of all the Versions of it, first and last, in all ages and in all languages, our Authorized English Version of it is confessedly one of the best. Many good people desire, and will accept, no other, preferring still to keep the old ancestral Book, reading the very words, in the very rhythm, with which they have been familiar from childhood.

Translators of the Bible are not inspired. The very Word of God, from which alone there is no appeal, is in Hebrew and Greek. Some portions of it are liturgical, and may be rendered with an eye to liturgical use. But all portions of it are incomparably sacred and precious; and our supreme duty in relation to it is to ascertain, if possible, and then to express, if possible, exactly its meaning, in every chapter and paragraph, in every sentence, in every idiom, and in every word. Rhythm may be studied, and old associations may be dealt with gently; but rhythm is only æsthetic, associations are accidental and changeable, and the most faithful renderings will finally be pronounced the best.

The feasibility of improving, and of greatly improving, the Authorized Version, is no longer an open question. Eleven years ago the task itself was undertaken with the expressed approbation, almost as it were by the commandment and authority, of the great bulk of English-speaking Christian people on both sides of the Atlantic, and all round the globe. During all these years some of the best Hebrew and Greek scholars in Great Britain and in the United States have bestowed their best endeavors upon this task. A portion of their work is now submitted to the intelligence and taste of the millions they have tried to serve. The Revised New Testament is before us, in a twofold form, Anglican and American. And our judgment is invoked concerning it.

This judgment must not be hasty. Nor will it, in the end, be passionate or prejudiced. Probably this Revision will not be accepted just as it is, in either form. But, in all the essentials of close and faithful rendering, it will be recognized as an immense improvement upon the King James Revision of nearly three hundred years

PREFACE.

ago, which must now begin to be laid aside. And as to the points of difference between the two Companies of Revisers, the renderings preferred by the American Revisers will, in most cases, be considered more exact and self-consistent than those preferred by their Anglican brethren.

Not much now remains to be done, compared with what has already been accomplished. Some better readings may be adopted, some awkwardly literal renderings may be improved, paragraphs may be shortened, remaining archaisms expelled, and rules, sometimes observed, may be observed throughout. With these emendations, so easy to make, we who speak the noblest of living languages may soon have the Book of books in a form very nearly perfect.

ROSWELL D. HITCHCOCK.

UNION THEOLOGICAL SEMINARY:
NEW YORK, *June* 28, 1881.

IN this second impression of the American Revised New Testament errors discovered in the first impression have been corrected. Special pains have been taken to make the Appendix both accurate and complete.

R. D. H.

August 10, 1881.

| Eng Revision. | K. James Vers. |

| THE GOSPEL ACCORDING TO | THE GOSPEL ACCORDING TO |
| **S. MARK.** | **ST. MARK.** |

CHAPTER I.

1 THE beginning of the gospel of Jesus Christ, [1] the Son of God.
2 Even as it is written [2] in Isaiah the prophet,
Behold, I send my messenger before thy face,
Who shall prepare thy way;
3 The voice of one crying in the wilderness,
Make ye ready the way of the Lord,
Make his paths straight;
4 John came, who baptized in the wilderness and preached the baptism of repentance unto remission of sins.
5 And there went out unto him all the country of Judæa, and all they of Jerusalem; and they were baptized of him in the river Jordan, confessing their sins.
6 And John was clothed with camel's hair, and *had* a leathern girdle about his loins, and did eat locusts and wild honey.
7 And he preached, saying, There cometh after me he that is mightier than I, the latchet of whose shoes I am not [3] worthy to stoop down and unloose.
8 I baptized you [4] with water; but he shall baptize you [4] with the [5] Holy Ghost.
9 And it came to pass in those days, that Jesus came from Nazareth of Galilee, and was baptized of John [6] in the Jordan.
10 And straightway coming up out of the water, he saw the heavens rent asunder, and the Spirit as a dove descending upon him: and a voice came out of the heavens, Thou art my beloved Son, in thee I am well pleased.
12 And straightway the Spirit driveth
13 him forth into the wilderness. And he was in the wilderness forty days tempted of Satan; and he was with the wild beasts; and the angels ministered unto him.
14 Now after that John was delivered

1 THE beginning of the gospel of Jesus Christ, the Son of God;
2 As it is written in the prophets, Behold, I send my messenger before thy face, which shall prepare thy way before thee.
3 The voice of one crying in the wilderness, Prepare ye the way of the Lord, make his paths straight.
4 John did baptize in the wilderness, and preach the baptism of repentance for the remission of sins.
5 And there went out unto him all the land of Judea, and they of Jerusalem, and were all baptized of him in the river of Jordan, confessing their sins.
6 And John was clothed with camel's hair, and with a girdle of a skin about his loins; and he did eat locusts and wild honey;
7 And preached, saying, There cometh one mightier than I after me, the latchet of whose shoes I am not worthy to stoop down and unloose.
8 I indeed have baptized you with water: but he shall baptize you with the Holy Ghost.
9 And it came to pass in those days, that Jesus came from Nazareth of Galilee, and was baptized of John in Jordan.
10 And straightway coming up out of the water, he saw the heavens opened, and the Spirit like a dove descending upon him:
11 And there came a voice from heaven, *saying*, Thou art my beloved Son, in whom I am well pleased.
12 And immediately the Spirit driveth him into the wilderness.
13 And he was there in the wilderness forty days tempted of Satan; and was with the wild beasts; and the angels ministered unto him.
14 Now after that John was put in

---

1 Some ancient authorities omit *the Son of God*.
2 Some ancient authorities read *in the prophets*.
3 Gr. *sufficient*.   4 Or, *in*
5 Or, *Holy Spirit*: and so throughout this book.
6 Gr. *into*.

American Version.

THE GOSPEL ACCORDING TO

MARK.

1 The beginning of the gospel of Jesus Christ, [1] the Son of God.
2 Even as it is written [2] in Isaiah the prophet,
Behold, I send my messenger before thy face,
Who shall prepare thy way;
3 The voice of one crying in the wilderness,
Make ye ready the way of the Lord,
Make his paths straight;
4 John came, who baptized in the wilderness and preached the baptism of repentance unto remission of sins.
5 And there went out unto him all the country of Judæa, and all they of Jerusalem; and they were baptized of him in the river Jordan, confessing their
6 sins. And John was clothed with camel's hair, and *had* a leathern girdle about his loins, and did eat
7 locusts and wild honey. And he preached, saying, There cometh after me he that is mightier than I, the latchet of whose shoes I am not [3] worthy to stoop
8 down and unloose. I baptized you [4] in water; but he shall baptize you [4] in the Holy Spirit.
9 And it came to pass in those days, that Jesus came from Nazareth of Galilee, and was baptized of John
10 [5] in the Jordan. And straightway coming up out of the water, he saw the heavens rent asunder, and the
11 Spirit as a dove descending upon him: and a voice came out of the heavens, Thou art my beloved Son, in thee I am well pleased.
12 And straightway the Spirit driveth him forth into the
13 wilderness. And he was in the wilderness forty days tempted of Satan; and he was with the wild beasts; and the angels ministered unto him.
14 Now after that John was delivered up, Jesus came

[1] Some ancient authorities omit *the Son of God.*
[2] Some ancient authorities read *in the prophets.*

[3] Gr. *sufficient.*
[4] Or, *with*

[5] Gr. *into.*

Eng. Revision.

up, Jesus came into Galilee, preach-
15 ing the gospel of God, and saying,
The time is fulfilled, and the kingdom
of God is at hand : repent ye, and believe in the gospel.
16 And passing along by the sea of
Galilee, he saw Simon and Andrew
the brother of Simon casting a net
in the sea: for they were fishers.
17 And Jesus said unto them, Come ye
after me, and I will make you to be-
18 come fishers of men. And straightway they left the nets, and followed
19 him. And going on a little further,
he saw James the *son* of Zebedee,
and John his brother, who also were
20 in the boat mending the nets. And
straightway he called them: and they
left their father Zebedee in the boat
with the hired servants, and went
after him.
21 And they go into Capernaum; and
straightway on the sabbath day he
entered into the synagogue and
22 taught. And they were astonished
at his teaching: for he taught them
as having authority, and not as the
23 scribes. And straightway there was
in their synagogue a man with an
unclean spirit; and he cried out,
24 saying, What have we to do with
thee, thou Jesus of Nazareth? art
thou come to destroy us? I know
thee who thou art, the Holy One of
25 God. And Jesus rebuked ¹ him, saying, Hold thy peace, and come out
26 of him. And the unclean spirit, ² tear-
ing him and crying with a loud voice,
27 came out of him. And they were
all amazed, insomuch that they questioned among themselves, saying,
What is this? a new teaching! with
authority he commandeth even the
unclean spirits, and they obey him.
28 And the report of him went out
straightway everywhere into all the
region of Galilee round about.
29 And straightway, ³ when they were
come out of the synagogue, they came
into the house of Simon and Andrew,
30 with James and John. Now Simon's
wife's mother lay sick of a fever; and
31 straightway they tell him of her : and
he came and took her by the hand,
and raised her up; and the fever left
her, and she ministered unto them.
32 And at even, when the sun did set,
they brought unto him all that were

---

1 Or, *it*
2 Or, *convulsing*
3 Some ancient authorities read *when he was come out of the synagogue, he came &c.*

K. James Vers.

prison, Jesus came into Galilee, preaching
the gospel of the kingdom of God,
15 And saying, The time is fulfilled, and
the kingdom of God is at hand: repent ye,
and believe the gospel.
16 Now as he walked by the sea of Galilee, he saw Simon and Andrew his brother
casting a net into the sea: for they were
fishers.
17 And Jesus said unto them, Come ye
after me, and I will make you to become
fishers of men.
18 And straightway they forsook their
nets, and followed him.
19 And when he had gone a little further
thence, he saw James the *son* of Zebedee,
and John his brother, who also were in the
ship mending their nets.
20 And straightway he called them: and
they left their father Zebedee in the ship
with the hired servants, and went after
him.
21 And they went into Capernaum; and
straightway on the sabbath day he entered
into the synagogue, and taught.
22 And they were astonished at his doctrine: for he taught them as one that had
authority, and not as the scribes.
23 And there was in their synagogue a
man with an unclean spirit; and he cried
out,
24 Saying, Let *us* alone ; what have
we to do with thee, thou Jesus of Nazareth? art thou come to destroy us? I
know thee who thou art, the Holy One of
God.
25 And Jesus rebuked him, saying,
Hold thy peace, and come out of him.
26 And when the unclean spirit had torn
him, and cried with a loud voice, he came
out of him.
27 And they were all amazed, insomuch
that they questioned among themselves,
saying, What thing is this? what new doctrine *is* this? for with authority commandeth he even the unclean spirits, and they
do obey him.
28 And immediately his fame spread
abroad throughout all the region round
about Galilee.
29 And forthwith, when they were come
out of the synagogue, they entered into
the house of Simon and Andrew, with
James and John.
30 But Simon's wife's mother lay sick
of a fever ; and anon they tell him of
her.
31 And he came and took her by the
hand, and lifted her up: and immediately
the fever left her, and she ministered unto
them.
32 And at even, when the sun did set,
they brought unto him all that were dis-

15 into Galilee, preaching the gospel of God, and saying, The time is fulfilled, and the kingdom of God is at hand: repent ye, and believe in the gospel.
16 And passing along by the sea of Galilee, he saw Simon and Andrew the brother of Simon casting a net
17 in the sea: for they were fishers. And Jesus said unto them, Come ye after me, and I will make you to be-
18 come fishers of men. And straightway they left the
19 nets, and followed him. And going on a little further, he saw James the *son* of Zebedee, and John his brother, who also were in the boat mending the nets.
20 And straightway he called them: and they left their father Zebedee in the boat with the hired servants, and went after him.
21 And they go into Capernaum; and straightway on the sabbath day he entered into the synagogue and
22 taught. And they were astonished at his teaching: for he taught them as having authority, and not as the
23 scribes. And straightway there was in their synagogue
24 a man with an unclean spirit; and he cried out, saying, What have we to do with thee, thou Jesus of Nazareth? art thou come to destroy us? I know thee
25 who thou art, the Holy One of God. And Jesus rebuked ¹him, saying, Hold thy peace, and come out
26 of him. And the unclean spirit, ²tearing him and
27 crying with a loud voice, came out of him. And they were all amazed, insomuch that they questioned among themselves, saying, What is this? a new teaching! with authority he commandeth even the unclean spirits,
28 and they obey him. And the report of him went out straightway everywhere into all the region of Galilee round about.
29 And straightway, ³when they were come out of the synagogue, they came into the house of Simon and
30 Andrew, with James and John. Now Simon's wife's mother lay sick of a fever; and straightway they tell
31 him of her: and he came and took her by the hand, and raised her up; and the fever left her, and she ministered unto them.
32 And at even, when the sun did set, they brought unto him all that were sick, and them that were

¹ Or, *it*
² Or, *convulsing*
³ Some ancient authorities read *when he was come out of the synagogue, he came &c.*

Eng. Revision. S. MARK. K. James Vers. 1. 32—

sick, and them that were [1] possessed 33 with devils. And all the city was 34 gathered together at the door. And he healed many that were sick with divers diseases, and cast out many [2] devils; and he suffered not the [2] devils to speak, because they knew him[3]. 35 And in the morning, a great while before day, he rose up and went out, and departed into a desert place, and 36 there prayed. And Simon and they that were with him followed after 37 him; and they found him, and say 38 unto him, All are seeking thee. And he saith unto them, Let us go elsewhere into the next towns, that I may preach there also; for to this 39 end came I forth. And he went into their synagogues throughout all Galilee, preaching and casting out [2] devils. 40 And there cometh to him a leper, beseeching him, [4] and kneeling down to him, and saying unto him, If thou 41 wilt, thou canst make me clean. And being moved with compassion, he stretched forth his hand, and touched him, and saith unto him, I will; be 42 thou made clean. And straightway the leprosy departed from him, and 43 he was made clean. And he [5] strictly charged him, and straightway sent 44 him out, and saith unto him, See thou say nothing to any man: but go thy way, shew thyself to the priest, and offer for thy cleansing the things which Moses commanded, for a testi- 45 mony unto them. But he went out, and began to publish it much, and to spread abroad the [6] matter, insomuch that [7] Jesus could no more openly enter into [8] a city, but was without in desert places: and they came to him from every quarter. 2 And when he entered again into Capernaum after some days, it was noised that he was [9] in the house. 2 And many were gathered together, so that there was no longer room for them, no, not even about the door: and he spake the word unto them. 3 And they come, bringing unto him a man sick of the palsy, borne of four. 4 And when they could not [10] come nigh unto him for the crowd, they uncovered the roof where he was: and when they had broken it up, they let down the bed whereon the sick of the 5 palsy lay. And Jesus seeing their faith saith unto the sick of the palsy, [11] Son,

eased, and them that were possessed with devils. 33 And all the city was gathered together at the door. 34 And he healed many that were sick of divers diseases, and cast out many devils; and suffered not the devils to speak, because they knew him. 35 And in the morning, rising up a great while before day, he went out, and departed into a solitary place, and there prayed. 36 And Simon and they that were with him followed after him. 37 And when they had found him, they said unto him, All men seek for thee. 38 And he said unto them, Let us go into the next towns, that I may preach there also: for therefore came I forth. 39 And he preached in their synagogues throughout all Galilee, and cast out devils. 40 And there came a leper to him, beseeching him, and kneeling down to him, and saying unto him, If thou wilt, thou canst make me clean. 41 And Jesus, moved with compassion, put forth *his* hand, and touched him, and saith unto him, I will; be thou clean. 42 And as soon as he had spoken, immediately the leprosy departed from him, and he was cleansed. 43 And he straitly charged him, and forthwith sent him away; 44 And saith unto him, See thou say nothing to any man: but go thy way, shew thyself to the priest, and offer for thy cleansing those things which Moses commanded, for a testimony unto them. 45 But he went out, and began to publish *it* much, and to blaze abroad the matter, insomuch that Jesus could no more openly enter into the city, but was without in desert places: and they came to him from every quarter.

CHAPTER II.

AND again he entered into Capernaum after *some* days; and it was noised that he was in the house.
2 And straightway many were gathered together, insomuch that there was no room to receive *them*, no, not so much as about the door: and he preached the word unto them.
3 And they come unto him, bringing one sick of the palsy, which was borne of four.
4 And when they could not come nigh unto him for the press, they uncovered the roof where he was: and when they had broken *it* up, they let down the bed wherein the sick of the palsy lay.
5 When Jesus saw their faith, he said unto the sick of the palsy, Son, thy sins be forgiven thee.

---
1 Or, *demoniacs*   2 Gr. *demons.*
3 Many ancient authorities add *to be Christ.* See Luke iv. 41.
4 Some ancient authorities omit *and kneeling down to him.*   5 Or, *sternly*   6 Gr. *word.*
7 Gr. *he.*   8 Or, *the city*   9 Or, *at home*
10 Many ancient authorities read *bring him unto him.*   11 Gr. *Child.*

33 possessed with demons. And all the city was gathered
34 together at the door. And he healed many that were
sick with divers diseases, and cast out many demons;
and he suffered not the demons to speak, because they
knew him².
35 And in the morning, a great while before day, he
rose up and went out, and departed into a desert
36 place, and there prayed. And Simon and they that
37 were with him followed after him; and they found him,
38 and say unto him, All are seeking thee. And he saith
unto them, Let us go elsewhere into the next towns,
that I may preach there also; for to this end came I
39 forth. And he went into their synagogues throughout
all Galilee, preaching and casting out demons.
40 And there cometh to him a leper, beseeching him,
³ and kneeling down to him, and saying unto him, If
41 thou wilt, thou canst make me clean. And being
moved with compassion, he stretched forth his hand,
and touched him, and saith unto him, I will; be thou
42 made clean. And straightway the leprosy departed
43 from him, and he was made clean. And he ⁴ strictly
44 charged him, and straightway sent him out, and
saith unto him, See thou say nothing to any man: but
go, shew thyself to the priest, and offer for thy
cleansing the things which Moses commanded, for a
45 testimony unto them. But he went out, and began
to publish it much, and to spread abroad the ⁵ matter,
insomuch that ⁶ Jesus could no more openly enter into
⁷ a city, but was without in desert places: and they
came to him from every quarter.

2 And when he entered again into Capernaum after
some days, it was noised that he was ⁸ in the house.
2 And many were gathered together, so that there was
no longer room *for them*, no, not even about the door:
3 and he spake the word unto them. And they come,
bringing unto him a man sick of the palsy, borne of
4 four. And when they could not ⁹ come nigh unto him
for the crowd, they uncovered the roof where he was:
and when they had broken it up, they let down the
5 ¹⁰ bed whereon the sick of the palsy lay. And Jesus
seeing their faith saith unto the sick of the palsy, ¹¹ Son,

¹ Or, *demoniacs*
² Many ancient authorities add *to be Christ*. See Luke iv. 41.
³ Some ancient authorities omit *and kneeling down to him*.
⁴ Or, *sternly*
⁵ Gr. *word*.
⁶ Gr. *he*.
⁷ Or, *the city*
⁸ Or, *at home*
⁹ Many ancient authorities read *bring him unto him*.
¹⁰ Or, *pallet*
¹¹ Gr. *Child*.

Eng. Revision. S. MARK. K. James Vers. 2. 5—

6 thy sins are forgiven. But there were certain of the scribes sitting there, and reasoning in their hearts,
7 Why doth this man thus speak? he blasphemeth: who can forgive
8 sins but one, *even* God? And straightway Jesus, perceiving in his spirit that they so reasoned within themselves, saith unto them, Why reason ye these things in your hearts?
9 Whether is easier, to say to the sick of the palsy, Thy sins are forgiven; or to say, Arise, and take up thy
10 bed, and walk? But that ye may know that the Son of man hath [1] power on earth to forgive sins (he
11 saith to the sick of the palsy), I say unto thee, Arise, take up thy bed,
12 and go unto thy house. And he arose, and straightway took up the bed, and went forth before them all; insomuch that they were all amazed, and glorified God, saying, We never saw it on this fashion.
13 And he went forth again by the sea side; and all the multitude resorted
14 unto him, and he taught them. And as he passed by, he saw Levi the *son* of Alphæus sitting at the place of toll, and he saith unto him, Follow me.
15 And he arose and followed him. And it came to pass, that he was sitting at meat in his house, and many [2] publicans and sinners sat down with Jesus and his disciples: for there were many, and
16 they followed him. And the scribes [3] of the Pharisees, when they saw that he was eating with the sinners and publicans, said unto his disciples, [4] He eateth [5] and drinketh with publicans
17 and sinners. And when Jesus heard it, he saith unto them, They that are [6] whole have no need of a physician, but they that are sick: I came not to call the righteous, but sinners.
18   And John's disciples and the Pharisees were fasting: and they come and say unto him, Why do John's disciples and the disciples of the Pharisees fast,
19 but thy disciples fast not? And Jesus said unto them, Can the sons of the bride-chamber fast, while the bridegroom is with them? as long as they have the bridegroom with them, they
20 cannot fast. But the days will come, when the bridegroom shall be taken away from them, and then will they
21 fast in that day. No man seweth a piece of undressed cloth on an old gar-

1 Or, *authority*
2 See marginal note on Matt. v. 46.
3 Some ancient authorities read *and the Pharisees*.
4 Or, How is it *that he eateth . . . sinners?*
5 Some ancient authorities omit *and drinketh.*
6 Gr. *strong.*

6 But there were certain of the scribes sitting there, and reasoning in their hearts,
7 Why doth this *man* thus speak blasphemies? who can forgive sins but God only?
8 And immediately, when Jesus perceived in his spirit that they so reasoned within themselves, he said unto them, Why reason ye these things in your hearts?
9 Whether is it easier to say to the sick of the palsy, *Thy* sins be forgiven thee; or to say, Arise, and take up thy bed, and walk?
10 But that ye may know that the Son of man hath power on earth to forgive sins, (he saith to the sick of the palsy,)
11 I say unto thee, Arise, and take up thy bed, and go thy way into thine house.
12 And immediately he arose, took up the bed, and went forth before them all; insomuch that they were all amazed, and glorified God, saying, We never saw it on this fashion.
13 And he went forth again by the sea side; and all the multitude resorted unto him, and he taught them.
14 And as he passed by, he saw Levi the *son* of Alpheus sitting at the receipt of custom, and said unto him, Follow me. And he arose and followed him.
15 And it came to pass, that, as Jesus sat at meat in his house, many publicans and sinners sat also together with Jesus and his disciples; for there were many, and they followed him.
16 And when the scribes and Pharisees saw him eat with publicans and sinners, they said unto his disciples, How is it that he eateth and drinketh with publicans and sinners?
17 When Jesus heard *it*, he saith unto them, They that are whole have no need of the physician, but they that are sick: I came not to call the righteous, but sinners to repentance.
18 And the disciples of John and of the Pharisees used to fast: and they come and say unto him, Why do the disciples of John and of the Pharisees fast, but thy disciples fast not?
19 And Jesus said unto them, Can the children of the bride-chamber fast, while the bridegroom is with them? as long as they have the bridegroom with them, they cannot fast.
20 But the days will come, when the bridegroom shall be taken away from them, and then shall they fast in those days.
21 No man also seweth a piece of new cloth on an old garment; else the new

6 thy sins are forgiven. But there were certain of the
  scribes sitting there, and reasoning in their hearts,
7 Why doth this man thus speak? he blasphemeth: who
8 can forgive sins but one, *even* God? And straightway Jesus, perceiving in his spirit that they so reasoned within themselves, saith unto them, Why reason
9 ye these things in your hearts? Whether is easier, to
  say to the sick of the palsy, Thy sins are forgiven: or
10 to say, Arise, and take up thy ¹bed, and walk? But
  that ye may know that the Son of man hath authority
  on earth to forgive sins (he saith to the sick of the
11 palsy), I say unto thee, Arise, take up thy ¹bed, and go
12 unto thy house. And he arose, and straightway took
  up the ¹bed, and went forth before them all; insomuch
  that they were all amazed, and glorified God, saying,
  We never saw it on this fashion.
13 And he went forth again by the sea side; and all
  the multitude resorted unto him, and he taught them.
14 And as he passed by, he saw Levi the *son* of Alphæus
  sitting at the place of toll, and he saith unto him,
15 Follow me. And he arose and followed him. And
  it came to pass, that he was sitting at meat in his
  house, and many ²publicans and sinners sat down with
  Jesus and his disciples: for there were many, and
16 they followed him. And the scribes ³ of the Pharisees,
  when they saw that he was eating with the sinners and
  publicans, said unto his disciples, ⁴He eateth ⁵and
17 drinketh with publicans and sinners. And when Jesus
  heard it, he saith unto them, They that are ⁶whole have
  no need of a physician, but they that are sick: I came
  not to call the righteous, but sinners.
18 And John's disciples and the Pharisees were fasting: and they come and say unto him, Why do John's
  disciples and the disciples of the Pharisees fast, but
19 thy disciples fast not? And Jesus said unto them,
  Can the sons of the bride-chamber fast, while the bridegroom is with them? as long as they have the bride-
20 groom with them, they cannot fast. But the days will
  come, when the bridegroom shall be taken away from
21 them, and then will they fast in that day. No man
  soweth a piece of undressed cloth on an old garment:

¹ Or, *pallet*

² See marginal note on Matt. v. 46.

³ Some ancient authorities read *and the Pharisees*.

⁴ Or, How is it *that he eateth . . . sinners?*

⁵ Some ancient authorities omit *and drinketh*.

⁶ Gr. *strong*.

Eng. Revision.

ment: else that which should fill it up taketh from it, the new from the old,
22 and a worse rent is made. And no man putteth new wine into old [1] wineskins: else the wine will burst the skins, and the wine perisheth, and the skins: but *they put* new wine into fresh wine-skins.
23 And it came to pass, that he was going on the sabbath day through the cornfields; and his disciples [2] began, as they went, to pluck the ears of
24 corn. And the Pharisees said unto him, Behold, why do they on the sabbath day that which is not lawful?
25 And he said unto them, Did ye never read what David did, when he had need, and was an hungred, he, and
26 they that were with him? How he entered into the house of God [3] when Abiathar was high priest, and did eat the shewbread, which it is not lawful to eat save for the priests, and gave
27 also to them that were with him? And he said unto them, The sabbath was made for man, and not man for the
28 sabbath: so that the Son of man is lord even of the sabbath.

3 And he entered again into the synagogue; and there was a man there
2 which had his hand withered. And they watched him, whether he would heal him on the sabbath day; that they
3 might accuse him. And he saith unto the man that had his hand withered,
4 [4] Stand forth. And he saith unto them, Is it lawful on the sabbath day to do good, or to do harm? to save a life, or to kill? But they held their peace.
5 And when he had looked round about on them with anger, being grieved at the hardening of their heart, he saith unto the man, Stretch forth thy hand. And he stretched it forth: and his hand
6 was restored. And the Pharisees went out, and straightway with the Herodians took counsel against him, how they might destroy him.
7 And Jesus with his disciples withdrew to the sea: and a great multitude from
8 Galilee followed: and from Judæa, and from Jerusalem, and from Idumæa, and beyond Jordan, and about Tyre and Sidon, a great multitude, hearing [5] what great things he did, came unto
9 him. And he spake to his disciples, that a little boat should wait on him because of the cr wd, lest they should

1 That is, *skins used as bottles.*
2 Gr. *began to make their way plucking.*
3 Some ancient authorities read *in the days of Abiathar the high priest.*
4 Gr. *Arise into the midst.*
5 Or, *all the things that he did*

S. MARK.

K. James Vers. 2. 21—

piece that filled it up taketh away from the old, and the rent is made worse.
22 And no man putteth new wine into old bottles; else the new wine doth burst the bottles, and the wine is spilled, and the bottles will be marred: but new wine must be put into new bottles.
23 And it came to pass, that he went through the corn fields on the sabbath day; and his disciples began, as they went, to pluck the ears of corn.
24 And the Pharisees said unto him, Behold, why do they on the sabbath day that which is not lawful?
25 And he said unto them, Have ye never read what David did, when he had need, and was a hungered, he, and they that were with him?
26 How he went into the house of God in the days of Abiathar the high priest, and did eat the shewbread, which is not lawful to eat but for the priests, and gave also to them which were with him?
27 And he said unto them, The sabbath was made for man, and not man for the sabbath:
28 Therefore the Son of man is Lord also of the sabbath.

CHAPTER III.

AND he entered again into the synagogue; and there was a man there which had a withered hand.
2 And they watched him, whether he would heal him on the sabbath day; that they might accuse him.
3 And he saith unto the man which had the withered hand, Stand forth.
4 And he saith unto them, Is it lawful to do good on the sabbath days, or to do evil? to save life, or to kill? But they held their peace.
5 And when he had looked round about on them with anger, being grieved for the hardness of their hearts, he saith unto the man, Stretch forth thine hand. And he stretched *it* out: and his hand was restored whole as the other.
6 And the Pharisees went forth, and straightway took counsel with the Herodians against him, how they might destroy him.
7 But Jesus withdrew himself with his disciples to the sea: and a great multitude from Galilee followed him, and from Judea,
8 And from Jerusalem, and from Idumea, and *from* beyond Jordan; and they about Tyre and Sidon, a great multitude, when they had heard what great things he did, came unto him.
9 And he spake to his disciples, that a small ship should wait on him because of

else that which should fill it up taketh from it, the new
22 from the old, and a worse rent is made. And no man putteth new wine into old ¹ wine-skins: else the wine will burst the skins, and the wine perisheth, and the skins: but *they put* new wine into fresh wine-skins.

23 And it came to pass, that he was going on the sabbath day through the cornfields; and his disciples
24 ² began, as they went, to pluck the ears of corn. And the Pharisees said unto him, Behold, why do they on
25 the sabbath day that which is not lawful? And he said unto them, Did ye never read what David did, when he had need, and was an hungred, he, and
26 they that were with him? How he entered into the house of God ³ when Abiathar was high priest, and did eat the shewbread, which it is not lawful to eat save for the priests, and gave also to them that were with
27 him? And he said unto them, The sabbath was made
28 for man, and not man for the sabbath: so that the Son of man is lord even of the sabbath.

3 And he entered again into the synagogue; and there
2 was a man there who had his hand withered. And they watched him, whether he would heal him on the
3 sabbath day; that they might accuse him. And he saith unto the man that had his hand withered, ⁴ Stand
4 forth. And he saith unto them, Is it lawful on the sabbath day to do good, or to do harm? to save a
5 life, or to kill? But they held their peace. And when he had looked round about on them with anger, being grieved at the hardening of their heart, he saith unto the man, Stretch forth thy hand. And he
6 stretched it forth: and his hand was restored. And the Pharisees went out, and straightway with the Herodians took counsel against him, how they might destroy him.

7 And Jesus with his disciples withdrew to the sea: and a great multitude from Galilee followed: and
8 from Judæa, and from Jerusalem, and from Idumæa, and beyond Jordan, and about Tyre and Sidon, a great multitude, hearing ⁵ what great things he did,
9 came unto him. And he spake to his disciples, that a little boat should wait on him because of the crowd,

¹ That is, skins used as *bottles*.
² Gr. *began to make* their *way plucking*.
³ Some ancient authorities read *in the days of Abiathar the high priest*.
⁴ Gr. *Arise into the midst*.
⁵ Or, *all the things that he did*

Eng. Revision.

10 throng him: for he had healed many; insomuch that as many as had ¹plagues ²pressed upon him that they might
11 touch him. And the unclean spirits, whensoever they beheld him, fell down before him, and cried, saying, Thou art
12 the Son of God. And he charged them much that they should not make him known.
13 And he goeth up into the mountain, and calleth unto him whom he himself
14 would: and they went unto him. And he appointed twelve, ³ that they might be with him, and that he might send
15 them forth to preach, and to have
16 authority to cast out ⁴devils: ⁵ and
17 Simon he surnamed Peter; and James the *son* of Zebedee, and John the brother of James; and them he surnamed Boanerges, which is, Sons of
18 thunder: and Andrew, and Philip, and Bartholomew, and Matthew, and Thomas, and James the *son* of Alphæus, and Thaddæus, and Simon the
19 ⁶Cananæan, and Judas Iscariot, which also betrayed him.
20 And he cometh ⁷ into a house. And the multitude cometh together again, so that they could not so much as eat
21 bread. And when his friends heard it, they went out to lay hold on him: for
22 they said, He is beside himself. And the scribes which came down from Jerusalem said, He hath Beelzebub, and, ⁸By the prince of the ⁴devils
23 casteth he out the ⁴devils. And he called them unto him, and said unto them in parables, How can Satan cast
24 out Satan? And if a kingdom be divided against itself, that kingdom cannot
25 stand. And if a house be divided against itself, that house will not be
26 able to stand. And if Satan hath risen up against himself, and is divided, he
27 cannot stand, but hath an end. But no one can enter into the house of the strong *man*, and spoil his goods, except he first bind the strong *man*; and then
28 he will spoil his house. Verily I say unto you, All their sins shall be forgiven unto the sons of men, and their blasphemies wherewith soever they
29 shall blaspheme: but whosoever shall blaspheme against the Holy Spirit hath never forgiveness, but is guilty of an
30 eternal sin: because they said, He hath an unclean spirit.

---

1 Gr. s*courges*.
2 Gr. *fell*.
3 Some ancient authorities add *whom also he named apostles*. See Luke vi. 13.
4 Gr. *demons*.
5 Some ancient authorities insert *and he appointed twelve*.
6 Or, *Zealot*. See Luke vi. 15; Acts i. 13.
7 Or, *home*
8 Or, *In*

S. MARK.

K. James Vers.

the multitude, lest they should throng him.
10 For he had healed many; insomuch that they pressed upon him for to touch him, as many as had plagues.
11 And unclean spirits, when they saw him, fell down before him, and cried, saying, Thou art the Son of God.
12 And he straitly charged them that they should not make him known.
13 And he goeth up into a mountain, and calleth *unto him* whom he would: and they came unto him.
14 And he ordained twelve, that they should be with him, and that he might send them forth to preach,
15 And to have power to heal sicknesses, and to cast out devils:
16 And Simon he surnamed Peter;
17 And James the *son* of Zebedee, and John the brother of James; and he surnamed them Boanerges, which is, The sons of thunder:
18 And Andrew, and Philip, and Bartholomew, and Matthew, and Thomas, and James the *son* of Alpheus, and Thaddeus, and Simon the Canaanite,
19 And Judas Iscariot, which also betrayed him: and they went into a house.
20 And the multitude cometh together again, so that they could not so much as eat bread.
21 And when his friends heard *of it*, they went out to lay hold on him: for they said, He is beside himself.
22 ¶ And the scribes which came down from Jerusalem said, He hath Beelzebub, and by the prince of the devils casteth he out devils.
23 And he called them *unto him*, and said unto them in parables, How can Satan cast out Satan?
24 And if a kingdom be divided against itself, that kingdom cannot stand.
25 And if a house be divided against itself, that house cannot stand.
26 And if Satan rise up against himself, and be divided, he cannot stand, but hath an end.
27 No man can enter into a strong man's house, and spoil his goods, except he will first bind the strong man; and then he will spoil his house.
28 Verily I say unto you, All sins shall be forgiven unto the sons of men, and blasphemies wherewith soever they shall blaspheme:
29 But he that shall blaspheme against the Holy Ghost hath never forgiveness, but is in danger of eternal damnation:
30 Because they said, He hath an unclean spirit.

10 lest they should throng him : for he had healed many; insomuch that as many as had ¹plagues ²pressed upon
11 him that they might touch him. And the unclean spirits, whensoever they beheld him, fell down before
12 him, and cried, saying, Thou art the Son of God. And he charged them much that they should not make him known.
13 And he goeth up into the mountain, and calleth unto him whom he himself would : and they went unto
14 him. And he appointed twelve,³ that they might be with him, and that he might send them forth to preach,
15
16 and to have authority to cast out demons : ⁴ and Simon he
17 surnamed Peter ; and James the *son* of Zebedee, and John the brother of James ; and them he surnamed
18 Boanerges, which is, Sons of thunder : and Andrew, and Philip, and Bartholomew, and Matthew, and Thomas, and James the *son* of Alphæus, and Thad-
19 dæus, and Simon the ⁵Cananæan, and Judas Iscariot, who also betrayed him.
20 And he cometh ⁶into a house. And the multitude cometh together again, so that they could not so much
21 as eat bread. And when his friends heard it, ·they went out to lay hold on him : for they said, He is
22 beside himself. And the scribes that came down from Jerusalem said, He hath Beelzebub, and, ⁷By the prince of the demons casteth he out the demons.
23 And he called them unto him, and said unto them in
24 parables, How can Satan cast out Satan? And if a kingdom be divided against itself, that kingdom cannot
25 stand. And if a house be divided against itself, that
26 house will not be able to stand. And if Satan hath risen up against himself, and is divided, he cannot
27 stand, but hath an end. But no one can enter into the house of the strong *man*, and spoil his goods, except he first bind the strong *man*; and then he will
28 spoil his house. Verily I say unto you, All their sins shall be forgiven unto the sons of men, and their blas-
29 phemies wherewith soever they shall blaspheme : but whosoever shall blaspheme against the Holy Spirit hath never forgiveness, but is guilty of an eternal sin :
30 because they said, He hath an unclean spirit.

¹ Gr. scourges.
² Gr. fell.
³ Some ancient authorities add *whom also he named apostles.* See Luke vi. 13.
⁴ Some ancient authorities insert *and he appointed twelve.*
⁵ Or, Zealot. See Luke vi. 15; Acts i 13.
⁶ Or, *home*
⁷ Or, *In*

Eng. Revision

31 And there come his mother and his brethren; and, standing without, they
32 sent unto him, calling him. And a multitude was sitting about him; and they say unto him, Behold, thy mother and thy brethren without seek for thee.
33 And he answereth them, and saith, Who
34 is my mother and my brethren? And looking round on them which sat round about him, he saith, Behold, my mother
35 and my brethren! For whosoever shall do the will of God, the same is my brother, and sister, and mother.

4 And again he began to teach by the sea side. And there is gathered unto him a very great multitude, so that he entered into a boat, and sat in the sea; and all the multitude were by the sea
2 on the land. And he taught them many things in parables, and said
3 unto them in his teaching, Hearken: Behold, the sower went forth to sow:
4 and it came to pass, as he sowed, some seed fell by the way side, and the birds
5 came and devoured it. And other fell on the rocky ground, where it had not much earth; and straightway it sprang up, because it had no deepness of earth:
6 and when the sun was risen, it was scorched; and because it had no root,
7 it withered away. And other fell among the thorns, and the thorns grew up, and choked it, and it yielded no fruit.
8 And others fell into the good ground, and yielded fruit, growing up and increasing; and brought forth, thirtyfold, and sixtyfold, and a hundredfold.
9 And he said, Who hath ears to hear, let him hear.
10 And when he was alone, they that were about him with the twelve asked
11 of him the parables. And he said unto them, Unto you is given the mystery of the kingdom of God: but unto them that are without, all things are done in
12 parables: that seeing they may see, and not perceive; and hearing they may hear, and not understand; lest haply they should turn again, and it
13 should be forgiven them. And he saith unto them, Know ye not this parable?
14 and how shall ye know all the parables?
15 The sower soweth the word. And these are they by the way side, where the word is sown; and when they have heard, straightway cometh Satan, and

K. James Vers.

31 ¶ There came then his brethren and his mother, and, standing without, sent unto him, calling him.
32 And the multitude sat about him, and they said unto him, Behold, thy mother and thy brethren without seek for thee.
33 And he answered them, saying, Who is my mother, or my brethren?
34 And he looked round about on them which sat about him, and said, Behold my mother and my brethren!
35 For whosoever shall do the will of God, the same is my brother, and my sister, and mother.

CHAPTER IV.

AND he began again to teach by the sea side: and there was gathered unto him a great multitude, so that he entered into a ship, and sat in the sea; and the whole multitude was by the sea on the land.
2 And he taught them many things by parables, and said unto them in his doctrine,
3 Hearken; Behold, there went out a sower to sow:
4 And it came to pass, as he sowed, some fell by the way side, and the fowls of the air came and devoured it up.
5 And some fell on stony ground, where it had not much earth; and immediately it sprang up, because it had no depth of earth:
6 But when the sun was up, it was scorched; and because it had no root, it withered away.
7 And some fell among thorns, and the thorns grew up, and choked it, and it yielded no fruit.
8 And other fell on good ground, and did yield fruit that sprang up and increased, and brought forth, some thirty, and some sixty, and some a hundred.
9 And he said unto them, He that hath ears to hear, let him hear.
10 And when he was alone, they that were about him with the twelve asked of him the parable.
11 And he said unto them, Unto you it is given to know the mystery of the kingdom of God: but unto them that are without, all *these* things are done in parables:
12 That seeing they may see, and not perceive; and hearing they may hear, and not understand; lest at any time they should be converted, and *their* sins should be forgiven them.
13 And he said unto them, Know ye not this parable? and how then will ye know all parables?
14 ¶ The sower soweth the word.
15 And these are they by the way side, where the word is sown; but when they have heard, Satan cometh immediately,

31 And there come his mother and his brethren; and, standing without, they sent unto him, calling him.
32 And a multitude was sitting about him; 'and they say unto him, Behold, thy mother and thy brethren with-
33 out seek for thee. And he answereth them, and saith,
34 Who is my mother and my brethren? And looking round on them that sat round about him, he saith,
35 Behold, my mother and my brethren! For whosoever shall do the will of God, the same is my brother, and sister, and mother.

4 And again he began to teach by the sea side. And there is gathered unto him a very great multitude, so that he entered into a boat, and sat in the sea; and all
2 the multitude were by the sea on the land. And he taught them many things in parables, and said unto
3 them in his teaching, Hearken: Behold, the sower
4 went forth to sow: and it came to pass, as he sowed, some *seed* fell by the way side, and the birds came and
5 devoured it. And other fell on the rocky *ground*, where it had not much earth; and straightway it
6 sprang up, because it had no deepness of earth: and when the sun was risen, it was scorched; and because
7 it had no root, it withered away. And other fell among the thorns, and the thorns grew up, and choked
8 it, and it yielded no fruit. And others fell into the good ground, and yielded fruit, growing up and increasing; and brought forth, thirtyfold, and sixtyfold,
9 and a hundredfold. And he said, Who hath ears to hear, let him hear.
10 And when he was alone, they that were about him
11 with the twelve asked of him the parables. And he said unto them, Unto you is given the mystery of the kingdom of God: but unto them that are without, all
12 things are done in parables: that seeing they may see, and not perceive; and hearing they may hear, and not understand; lest haply they should turn again, and it
13 should be forgiven them. And he saith unto them, Know ye not this parable? and how shall ye know all
14 the parables? The sower soweth the word. And
15 these are they by the way side, where the word is sown; and when they have heard, straightway cometh

Eng. Revision.

taketh away the word which hath been sown in them. And these in like manner are they that are sown upon the rocky *places*, who, when they have heard the word, straightway receive it with joy; and they have no root in themselves, but endure for a while; then, when tribulation or persecution ariseth because of the word, straightway they stumble. And others are they that are sown among the thorns; these are they that have heard the word, and the cares of the [1] world, and the deceitfulness of riches, and the lusts of other things entering in, choke the word, and it becometh unfruitful.
20 And those are they that were sown upon the good ground; such as hear the word, and accept it, and bear fruit, thirtyfold, and sixtyfold, and a hundredfold.
21 And he said unto them, Is the lamp brought to be put under the bushel, or under the bed, *and* not to be put on the stand? For there is nothing hid, save that it should be manifested; neither was *anything* made secret, but that it should come to light. If any man hath ears to hear, let him hear. And he said unto them, Take heed what ye hear: with what measure ye mete it shall be measured unto you: and more shall be given unto you. For he that hath, to him shall be given: and he that hath not, from him shall be taken away even that which he hath.
26 And he said, So is the kingdom of God, as if a man should cast seed upon the earth; and should sleep and rise night and day, and the seed should spring up and grow, he knoweth not how. The earth [2] beareth fruit of herself; first the blade, then the ear, then the full corn in the ear. But when the fruit [3] is ripe, straightway he [4] putteth forth the sickle, because the harvest is come.
30 And he said, How shall we liken the kingdom of God? or in what parable shall we set it forth? [5] It is like a grain of mustard seed, which, when it is sown upon the earth, though it be less than all the seeds that are upon the earth, yet when it is sown, groweth up, and becometh greater than all the herbs, and putteth out great branches;

1 Or, *age*
2 Or, *yieldeth*
3 Or, *alloweth*
4 Or, *sendeth forth*
5 Gr. *As unto*.

S. MARK.   K. James Vers.   4. 15—

and taketh away the word that was sown in their hearts.
16 And these are they likewise which are sown on stony ground; who, when they have heard the word, immediately receive it with gladness;
17 And have no root in themselves, and so endure but for a time: afterward when affliction or persecution ariseth for the word's sake, immediately they are offended.
18 And these are they which are sown among thorns; such as hear the word,
19 And the cares of this world, and the deceitfulness of riches, and the lusts of other things entering in, choke the word, and it becometh unfruitful.
20 And these are they which are sown on good ground; such as hear the word, and receive *it*, and bring forth fruit, some thirtyfold, some sixty, and some a hundred.
21 ¶ And he said unto them, Is a candle brought to be put under a bushel, or under a bed? and not to be set on a candlestick?
22 For there is nothing hid, which shall not be manifested; neither was any thing kept secret, but that it should come abroad.
23 If any man have ears to hear, let him hear.
24 And he said unto them, Take heed what ye hear. With what measure ye mete, it shall be measured to you: and unto you that hear shall more be given.
25 For he that hath, to him shall be given; and he that hath not, from him shall be taken even that which he hath.
26 ¶ And he said, So is the kingdom of God, as if a man should cast seed into the ground;
27 And should sleep, and rise night and day, and the seed should spring and grow up, he knoweth not how.
28 For the earth bringeth forth fruit of herself; first the blade, then the ear, after that the full corn in the ear.
29 But when the fruit is brought forth, immediately he putteth in the sickle, because the harvest is come.
30 ¶ And he said, Whereunto shall we liken the kingdom of God? or with what comparison shall we compare it?
31 *It is* like a grain of mustard seed, which, when it is sown in the earth, less than all the seeds that be in the earth.
32 But when it is sown, it groweth up, and becometh greater than all herbs, and shooteth out great branches; so that the

Satan, and taketh away the word which hath been
16 sown in them. And these in like manner are they
that are sown upon the rocky *places*, who, when they
have heard the word, straightway receive it with joy;
17 and they have no root in themselves, but endure for a
while; then, when tribulation or persecution ariseth
18 because of the word, straightway they stumble. And
others are they that are sown among the thorns;
19 these are they that have heard the word, and the cares
of the ¹ world, and the deceitfulness of riches, and the
lusts of other things entering in, choke the word, and
20 it becometh unfruitful. And those are they that were
sown upon the good ground; such as hear the word,
and accept it, and bear fruit, thirtyfold, and sixtyfold,
and a hundredfold.

¹ Or, *age*

21   And he said unto them, Is the lamp brought to be
put under the bushel, or under the bed, *and* not to be
22 put on the stand? For there is nothing hid, save that
it should be manifested; neither was *anything* made
23 secret, but that it should come to light. If any man
24 hath ears to hear, let him hear. And he said unto
them, Take heed what ye hear: with what measure ye
mete it shall be measured unto you: and more shall
25 be given unto you. For he that hath, to him shall be
given: and he that hath not, from him shall be taken
away even that which he hath.

26   And he said, So is the kingdom of God, as if a man
27 should cast seed upon the earth; and should sleep
and rise night and day, and the seed should spring up
28 and grow, he knoweth not how. The earth ² beareth
fruit of herself; first the blade, then the ear, then the
29 full corn in the ear. But when the fruit ³ is ripe,
straightway he ⁴ putteth forth the sickle, because the
harvest is come.

² Or, *yieldeth*

³ Or, *alloweth*

⁴ Or, *sendeth forth*

30   And he said, How shall we liken the kingdom of
31 God? or in what parable shall we set it forth? ⁵ It is
like a grain of mustard seed, which, when it is sown
upon the earth, though it be less than all the seeds
32 that are upon the earth, yet when it is sown,
groweth up, and becometh greater than all the
herbs, and putteth out great branches; so that the

⁵ Gr. *As unto.*

Eng. Revision.   S. MARK.   K. James Vers.

so that the birds of the heaven can lodge under the shadow thereof.
33 And with many such parables spake he the word unto them, as they were
34 able to hear it: and without a parable spake he not unto them: but privately to his own disciples he expounded all things.
35 And on that day, when even was come, he saith unto them, Let us go
36 over unto the other side. And leaving the multitude, they take him with them, even as he was, in the boat.
37 And other boats were with him. And there ariseth a great storm of wind, and the waves beat into the boat. insomuch that the boat was now filling.
38 And he himself was in the stern, asleep on the cushion: and they awake him, and say unto him, ¹ Master, carest thou
39 not that we perish? And he awoke, and rebuked the wind, and said unto the sea, Peace, be still. And the wind ceased, and there was a great calm.
40 And he said unto them, Why are ye
41 fearful? have ye not yet faith? And they feared exceedingly, and said one to another, Who then is this, that even the wind and the sea obey him?
5 And they came to the other side of the sea, into the country of the Gera-
2 senes. And when he was come out of the boat, straightway there met him out of the tombs a man with an un-
3 clean spirit, who had his dwelling in the tombs: and no man could any more
4 bind him, no, not with a chain; because that he had been often bound with fetters and chains, and the chains had been rent asunder by him, and the fetters broken in pieces: and no
5 man had strength to tame him. And always, night and day, in the tombs and in the mountains, he was crying out, and cutting himself with stones.
6 And when he saw Jesus from afar, he
7 ran and worshipped him; and crying out with a loud voice, he saith, What have I to do with thee, Jesus, thou Son of the Most High God? I adjure thee
8 by God, torment me not. For he said unto him, Come forth, thou unclean
9 spirit, out of the man. And he asked him, What is thy name? and he saith unto him, My name is Legion; for we
10 are many. And he besought him much that he would not send them

¹ Or, *Teacher*

fowls of the air may lodge under the shadow of it.
33 And with many such parables spake he the word unto them, as they were able to hear it.
34 But without a parable spake he not unto them: and when they were alone, he expounded all things to his disciples.
35 And the same day, when the even was come, he saith unto them, Let us pass over unto the other side.
36 And when they had sent away the multitude, they took him even as he was in the ship. And there were also with him other little ships.
37 And there arose a great storm of wind, and the waves beat into the ship, so that it was now full.
38 And he was in the hinder part of the ship, asleep on a pillow: and they awake him, and say unto him, Master, carest thou not that we perish?
39 And he arose, and rebuked the wind, and said unto the sea, Peace, be still. And the wind ceased, and there was a great calm.
40 And he said unto them, Why are ye so fearful? how is it that ye have no faith?
41 And they feared exceedingly, and said one to another, What manner of man is this, that even the wind and the sea obey him?

CHAPTER V.

AND they came over unto the other side of the sea, into the country of the Gadarenes.
2 And when he was come out of the ship, immediately there met him out of the tombs a man with an unclean spirit,
3 Who had *his* dwelling among the tombs; and no man could bind him, no, not with chains:
4 Because that he had been often bound with fetters and chains, and the chains had been plucked asunder by him, and the fetters broken in pieces: neither could any *man* tame him.
5 And always, night and day, he was in the mountains, and in the tombs, crying, and cutting himself with stones.
6 But when he saw Jesus afar off, he ran and worshipped him,
7 And cried with a loud voice, and said, What have I to do with thee, Jesus, *thou* Son of the most high God? I adjure thee by God, that thou torment me not.
8 (For he said unto him, Come out of the man, *thou* unclean spirit.)
9 And he asked him, What *is* thy name? And he answered, saying, My name *is* Legion: for we are many.
10 And he besought him much that he would not send them away out of the country.

birds of the heaven can lodge under the shadow thereof.

33 And with many such parables spake he the word 34 unto them, as they were able to hear it: and without a parable spake he not unto them: but privately to his own disciples he expounded all things.

35 And on that day, when even was come, he saith 36 unto them, Let us go over unto the other side. And leaving the multitude, they take him with them, even as he was, in the boat. And other boats were with 37 him. And there ariseth a great storm of wind, and the waves beat into the boat, insomuch that the boat 38 was now filling. And he himself was in the stern, asleep on the cushion: and they awake him, and say unto 39 him, ¹Master, carest thou not that we perish? And ¹ Or, *Teacher* he awoke, and rebuked the wind, and said unto the sea, Peace, be still. And the wind ceased, and there 40 was a great calm. And he said unto them, Why are 41 ye fearful? have ye not yet faith? And they feared exceedingly, and said one to another, Who then is this, that even the wind and the sea obey him?

5 And they came to the other side of the sea, into the 2 country of the Gerasenes. And when he was come out of the boat, straightway there met him out of the 3 tombs a man with an unclean spirit, who had his dwelling in the tombs: and no man could any more 4 bind him, no, not with a chain; because that he had been often bound with fetters and chains, and the chains had been rent asunder by him, and the fetters broken in pieces: and no man had strength to tame 5 him. And always, night and day, in the tombs and in the mountains, he was crying out, and cutting himself 6 with stones. And when he saw Jesus from afar, he 7 ran and worshipped him; and crying out with a loud voice, he saith, What have I to do with thee, Jesus, thou Son of the Most High God? I adjure thee by 8 God, torment me not. For he said unto him, Come 9 forth, thou unclean spirit, out of the man. And he asked him, What is thy name? And he saith unto 10 him, My name is Legion; for we are many. And he besought him much that he would not send them

Eng. Revision	K. James Vers.
11 away out of the country. Now there was there on the mountain side a great 12 herd of swine feeding. And they besought him, saying, Send us into the swine, that we may enter into them. 13 And he gave them leave. And the unclean spirits came out, and entered into the swine: and the herd rushed down the steep into the sea, *in number* about two thousand; and they were 14 choked in the sea. And they that fed them fled, and told it in the city, and in the country. And they came to see what it was that had come to pass. 15 And they come to Jesus, and behold ¹him that was possessed with devils sitting, clothed and in his right mind, 16 *even* him that had the legion: and they were afraid. And they that saw it declared unto them how it befell ¹him that was possessed with devils, and 17 concerning the swine. And they began to beseech him to depart from their 18 borders. And as he was entering into the boat, he that had been possessed with ²devils besought him that he 19 might be with him. And he suffered him not, but saith unto him, Go to thy house unto thy friends, and tell them how great things the Lord hath done for thee, and *how* he had mercy on 20 thee. And he went his way, and began to publish in Decapolis how great things Jesus had done for him: and all men did marvel. 21 And when Jesus had crossed over again in the boat unto the other side, a great multitude was gathered unto 22 him: and he was by the sea. And there cometh one of the rulers of the synagogue, Jaïrus by name; and see- 23 ing him, he falleth at his feet, and beseecheth him much, saying, My little daughter is at the point of death: *I pray thee*, that thou come and lay thy hands on her, that she may be ³made 24 whole, and live. And he went with him; and a great multitude followed him, and they thronged him. 25 And a woman, which had an issue of 26 blood twelve years, and had suffered many things of many physicians, and had spent all that she had, and was nothing bettered, but rather grew 27 worse, having heard the things concerning Jesus, came in the crowd be- 28 hind, and touched his garment. For she said, If I touch but his garments, I	11 Now there was there nigh unto the mountains a great herd of swine feeding. 12 And all the devils besought him, saying, Send us into the swine, that we may enter into them. 13 And forthwith Jesus gave them leave. And the unclean spirits went out, and entered into the swine; and the herd ran violently down a steep place into the sea, (they were about two thousand,) and were choked in the sea. 14 And they that fed the swine fled, and told *it* in the city, and in the country. And they went out to see what it was that was done. 15 And they come to Jesus, and see him that was possessed with the devil, and had the legion, sitting, and clothed, and in his right mind; and they were afraid. 16 And they that saw *it* told them how it befell to him that was possessed with the devil, and *also* concerning the swine. 17 And they began to pray him to depart out of their coasts. 18 And when he was come into the ship, he that had been possessed with the devil prayed him that he might be with him. 19 Howbeit Jesus suffered him not, but saith unto him, Go home to thy friends, and tell them how great things the Lord hath done for thee, and hath had compassion on thee. 20 And he departed, and began to publish in Decapolis how great things Jesus had done for him: and all *men* did marvel. 21 And when Jesus was passed over again by ship unto the other side, much people gathered unto him; and he was nigh unto the sea. 22 And, behold, there cometh one of the rulers of the synagogue, Jairus by name; and when he saw him, he fell at his feet, 23 And besought him greatly, saying, My little daughter lieth at the point of death: *I pray thee*, come and lay thy hands on her, that she may be healed; and she shall live. 24 And *Jesus* went with him; and much people followed him, and thronged him. 25 And a certain woman, which had an issue of blood twelve years, 26 And had suffered many things of many physicians, and had spent all that she had, and was nothing bettered, but rather grew worse, 27 When she had heard of Jesus, came in the press behind, and touched his garment. 28 For she said, If I may touch but his clothes, I shall be whole.

1 Or, *the demoniac*
2 Gr. *demons.*
3 Or, *saved*

11 away out of the country. Now there was there on the
12 mountain side a great herd of swine feeding. And
they besought him, saying, Send us into the swine,
13 that we may enter into them. And he gave them
leave. And the unclean spirits came out, and entered
into the swine: and the herd rushed down the steep
into the sea, *in number* about two thousand; and they
14 were choked in the sea. And they that fed them fled,
and told it in the city, and in the country. And they
15 came to see what it was that had come to pass. And
they come to Jesus, and behold [1] him that was pos- [1] Or,
sessed with demons sitting, clothed and in his right *the demoniac*
mind, *even* him that had the legion: and they were
16 afraid. And they that saw it declared unto them how
it befell [1] him that was possessed with demons, and con-
17 cerning the swine. And they began to beseech him to
18 depart from their borders. And as he was entering
into the boat, he that had been possessed with demons
19 besought him that he might be with him. And he
suffered him not, but saith unto him, Go to thy house
unto thy friends, and tell them how great things the
Lord hath done for thee, and *how* he had mercy on
20 thee. And he went his way, and began to publish in
Decapolis how great things Jesus had done for him:
and all men did marvel.

21 And when Jesus had crossed over again in the boat
unto the other side, a great multitude was gathered
22 unto him: and he was by the sea. And there cometh
one of the rulers of the synagogue, Jaïrus by name;
23 and seeing him, he falleth at his feet, and beseecheth
him much, saying, My little daughter is at the point
of death: *I pray thee*, that thou come and lay thy
hands on her, that she may be [2] made whole, and live. [2] Or, *saved*
24 And he went with him; and a great multitude fol-
lowed him, and they thronged him.

25 And a woman, who had an issue of blood twelve
26 years, and had suffered many things of many phy-
sicians, and had spent all that she had, and was nothing
27 bettered, but rather grew worse, having heard the
things concerning Jesus, came in the crowd behind,
28 and touched his garment. For she said, If I touch

Eng. Revision.	K. James Vers.

Eng. Revision.

29 shall be ¹made whole. And straightway the fountain of her blood was dried up; and she felt in her body that
30 she was healed of her ²plague. And straightway Jesus, perceiving in himself that the power *proceeding* from him had gone forth, turned him about in the crowd, and said, Who touched
31 my garments? And his disciples said unto him, Thou seest the multitude thronging thee, and sayest thou, Who
32 touched me? And he looked round about to see her that had done this
33 thing. But the woman fearing and trembling, knowing what had been done to her, came and fell down before
34 him, and told him all the truth. And he said unto her, Daughter, thy faith hath ³made thee whole; go in peace, and be whole of thy ²plague.
35 While he yet spake, they come from the ruler of the synagogue's *house*, saying, Thy daughter is dead: why troublest thou the ⁴Master any further?
36 But Jesus, ⁵not heeding the word spoken, saith unto the ruler of the synagogue, Fear not, only believe.
37 And he suffered no man to follow with him, save Peter, and James, and John
38 the brother of James. And they come to the house of the ruler of the synagogue; and he beholdeth a tumult, and *many* weeping and wailing greatly.
39 And when he was entered in, he saith unto them, Why make ye a tumult, and weep? the child is not dead, but
40 sleepeth. And they laughed him to scorn. But he, having put them all forth, taketh the father of the child and her mother and them that were with him, and goeth in where the child
41 was. And taking the child by the hand, he saith unto her, Talitha cumi; which is, being interpreted, Damsel, I
42 say unto thee, Arise. And straightway the damsel rose up, and walked; for she was twelve years old. And they were amazed straightway with a
43 great amazement. And he charged them much that no man should know this: and he commanded that *something* should be given her to eat.

6 And he went out from thence; and he cometh into his own country; and
2 his disciples follow him. And when the sabbath was come, he began to

---

1 Or, *saved*
2 Gr. *scourge*.
3 Or, *saved thee*
4 Or, *Teacher*
5 Or, *overhearing*

K. James Vers.

29 And straightway the fountain of her blood was dried up; and she felt in *her* body that she was healed of that plague.
30 And Jesus, immediately knowing in himself that virtue had gone out of him, turned him about in the press, and said, Who touched my clothes?
31 And his disciples said unto him, Thou seest the multitude thronging thee, and sayest thou, Who touched me?
32 And he looked round about to see her that had done this thing.
33 But the woman fearing and trembling, knowing what was done in her, came and fell down before him, and told him all the truth.
34 And he said unto her, Daughter, thy faith hath made thee whole; go in peace, and be whole of thy plague.
35 While he yet spake, there came from the ruler of the synagogue's *house* certain which said, Thy daughter is dead; why troublest thou the Master any further?
36 As soon as Jesus heard the word that was spoken, he saith unto the ruler of the synagogue, Be not afraid, only believe.
37 And he suffered no man to follow him, save Peter, and James, and John the brother of James.
38 And he cometh to the house of the ruler of the synagogue, and seeth the tumult, and them that wept and wailed greatly.
39 And when he was come in, he saith unto them, Why make ye this ado, and weep? the damsel is not dead, but sleepeth.
40 And they laughed him to scorn. But when he had put them all out, he taketh the father and the mother of the damsel, and them that were with him, and entereth in where the damsel was lying.
41 And he took the damsel by the hand, and said unto her, Talitha cumi; which is being interpreted, Damsel, (I say unto thee,) arise.
42 And straightway the damsel arose and walked; for she was *of the age o*' twelve years. And they were astonished with a great astonishment.
43 And he charged them straitly that no man should know it; and commanded that something should be given her to eat.

CHAPTER VI.

AND he went out from thence, and came into his own country; and his disciples follow him.
2 And when the sabbath day was come he began to teach in the synagogue: an

29 but his garments, I shall be ¹made whole. And straight- ¹ Or, *saved*
way the fountain of her blood was dried up; and she
felt in her body that she was healed of her ²plague. ² Gr. *scourge*.
30 And straightway Jesus, perceiving in himself that the
power *proceeding* from him had gone forth, turned
him about in the crowd, and said, Who touched my
31 garments? And his disciples said unto him, Thou
seest the multitude thronging thee, and sayest thou,
32 Who touched me? And he looked round about to
33 see her that had done this thing. But the woman
fearing and trembling, knowing what had been done to
her, came and fell down before him, and told him all
34 the truth. And he said unto her, Daughter, thy faith
hath ³made thee whole; go in peace, and be whole of ³ Or, *saved thee*
thy ²plague.
35 While he yet spake, they come from the ruler of the
synagogue's *house*, saying, Thy daughter is dead: why
36 troublest thou the ⁴Master any further? But Jesus, ⁴ Or, *Teacher*
⁵not heeding the word spoken, saith unto the ruler of ⁵ Or, *overhearing*
37 the synagogue, Fear not, only believe. And he suf-
fered no man to follow with him, save Peter, and
38 James, and John the brother of James. And they
come to the house of the ruler of the synagogue; and
he beholdeth a tumult, and *many* weeping and wailing
39 greatly. And when he was entered in, he saith unto
them, Why make ye a tumult, and weep? the child is
40 not dead, but sleepeth. And they laughed him to
scorn. But he, having put them all forth, taketh the
father of the child and her mother and them that were
41 with him, and goeth in where the child was. And
taking the child by the hand, he saith unto her, Talitha
cumi; which is, being interpreted, Damsel, I say unto
42 thee, Arise. And straightway the damsel rose up, and
walked; for she was twelve years old. And they were
43 amazed straightway with a great amazement. And he
charged them much that no man should know this:
and he commanded that *something* should be given her
to eat.

6 And he went out from thence; and he cometh into
2 his own country; and his disciples follow him. And
when the sabbath was come, he began to teach in the

Eng. Revision. — S. MARK. — K. James Vers.

teach in the synagogue: and [1] many hearing him were astonished, saying, Whence hath this man these things? and, What is the wisdom that is given unto this man, and *what mean* such [2] mighty works wrought by his hands?
3 Is not this the carpenter, the son of Mary, and brother of James, and Joses, and Judas, and Simon? and are not his sisters here with us? And they
4 were [3] offended in him. And Jesus said unto them, A prophet is not without honour, save in his own country, and among his own kin, and in his own
5 house. And he could there do no [4] mighty work, save that he laid his hands upon a few sick folk, and healed
6 them. And he marvelled because of their unbelief.
And he went round about the villages teaching.
7 And he called unto him the twelve, and began to send them forth by two and two; and he gave them authority
8 over the unclean spirits; and he charged them that they should take nothing for *their* journey, save a staff only; no bread, no wallet, no [5] money in their
9 [6] purse; but *to go* shod with sandals: and, *said he*, put not on two coats.
10 And he said unto them, Wheresoever ye enter into a house, there abide till
11 ye depart thence. And whatsoever place shall not receive you, and they hear you not, as ye go forth thence, shake off the dust that is under your
12 feet for a testimony unto them. And they went out, and preached that men
13 should repent. And they cast out many [7] devils, and anointed with oil many that were sick, and healed them.
14 And king Herod heard *thereof*; for his name had become known: and [8] he said, John [9] the Baptist is risen from the dead, and therefore do these pow-
15 ers work in him. But others said, It is Elijah. And others said, *It is* a proph-
16 et, *even* as one of the prophets. But Herod, when he heard *thereof*, said, John, whom I beheaded, he is risen.
17 For Herod himself had sent forth and laid hold upon John, and bound him in prison for the sake of Herodias, his brother Philip's wife: for he had mar-
18 ried her. For John said unto Herod, It is not lawful for thee to have thy
19 brother's wife. And Herodias set her-

1 Some ancient authorities insert *the.*
2 Gr. *powers.*
3 Gr. *caused to stumble.*
4 Gr. *power.*
5 Gr. *brass.*
6 Gr. *girdle.*
7 Gr. *demons.*
8 Some ancient authorities read *they.*
9 Gr. *the Baptizer.*

many hearing *him* were astonished, saying, From whence hath this *man* these things? and what wisdom *is* this which is given unto him, that even such mighty works are wrought by his hands?
3 Is not this the carpenter, the son of Mary, the brother of James, and Joses, and of Juda, and Simon? and are not his sisters here with us? And they were offended at him.
4 But Jesus said unto them, A prophet is not without honour, but in his own country, and among his own kin, and in his own house.
5 And he could there do no mighty work, save that he laid his hands upon a few sick folk, and healed *them*.
6 And he marvelled because of their unbelief. And he went round about the villages, teaching.
7 ¶ And he called *unto him* the twelve, and began to send them forth by two and two; and gave them power over unclean spirits;
8 And commanded them that they should take nothing for *their* journey, save a staff only; no scrip, no bread, no money in *their* purse;
9 But *be* shod with sandals; and not put on two coats.
10 And he said unto them, In what place soever ye enter into a house, there abide till ye depart from that place.
11 And whosoever shall not receive you, nor hear you, when ye depart thence, shake off the dust under your feet for a testimony against them. Verily I say unto you, It shall be more tolerable for Sodom and Gomorrah in the day of judgment, than for that city.
12 And they went out, and preached that men should repent.
13 And they cast out many devils, and anointed with oil many that were sick, and healed *them*.
14 And king Herod heard *of him;* (for his name was spread abroad;) and he said, That John the Baptist was risen from the dead, and therefore mighty works do shew forth themselves in him.
15 Others said, That it is Elias. And others said, That it is a prophet, or as one of the prophets.
16 But when Herod heard *thereof*, he said, It is John, whom I beheaded: he is risen from the dead.
17 For Herod himself had sent forth and laid hold upon John, and bound him in prison for Herodias' sake, his brother Philip's wife: for he had married her.
18 For John had said unto Herod, It is not lawful for thee to have thy brother's wife.
19 Therefore Herodias had a quarrel

synagogue: and ¹many hearing him were astonished, saying, Whence hath this man these things? and, What is the wisdom that is given unto this man, and *what mean* such ²mighty works wrought by his 3 hands? Is not this the carpenter, the son of Mary, and brother of James, and Joses, and Judas, and Simon? and are not his sisters here with us? And 4 they were ³offended in him. And Jesus said unto them, A prophet is not without honour, save in his own country, and among his own kin, and in his own house. 5 And he could there do no ⁴mighty work, save that he laid his hands upon a few sick folk, and healed 6 them. And he marvelled because of their unbelief.

And he went round about the villages teaching.
7 And he called unto him the twelve, and began to send them forth by two and two; and he gave them 8 authority over the unclean spirits; and he charged them that they should take nothing for *their* journey, save a staff only; no bread, no wallet, no ⁵money in 9 their ⁶purse; but *to go* shod with sandals: and, *said* 10 *he*, put not on two coats. And he said unto them, Wheresoever ye enter into a house, there abide till ye 11 depart thence. And whatsoever place shall not receive you, and they hear you not, as ye go forth thence, shake off the dust that is under your feet for a testi-12 mony unto them. And they went out, and preached 13 that *men* should repent. And they cast out many demons, and anointed with oil many that were sick, and healed them.
14 And king Herod heard *thereof*; for his name had become known: and ⁷he said, John ⁸the Baptist is risen from the dead, and therefore do these powers 15 work in him. But others said, It is Elijah. And others said, *It is* a prophet, *even* as one of the prophets. 16 But Herod, when he heard *thereof*, said, John, whom I 17 beheaded, he is risen. For Herod himself had sent forth and laid hold upon John, and bound him in prison for the sake of Herodias, his brother Philip's 18 wife: for he had married her. For John said unto Herod, It is not lawful for thee to have thy bro-19 ther's wife. And Herodias set herself against him, and

¹ Some ancient authorities insert *the*.
² Gr. *powers*.
³ Gr. *caused to stumble*.
⁴ Gr. *power*.
⁵ Gr. *brass*.
⁶ Gr. *girdle*.
⁷ Some ancient authorities read *they*.
⁸ Gr. *the Baptizer*.

Eng. Revision

20 self against him, and desired to kill him; and she could not; for Herod feared John, knowing that he was a righteous man and a holy, and kept him safe. And when he heard him, he was much perplexed[1]; and he heard
21 him gladly. And when a convenient day was come, that Herod on his birthday made a supper to his lords, and the [2] high captains, and the chief men
22 of Galilee; and when [3] the daughter of Herodias herself came in and danced, [4] she pleased Herod and them that sat at meat with him; and the king said unto the damsel, Ask of me whatsoever
23 thou wilt, and I will give it thee. And he sware unto her, Whatsoever thou shalt ask of me, I will give it thee, unto
24 the half of my kingdom. And she went out, and said unto her mother, What shall I ask? And she said, The head of
25 John [5] the Baptist. And she came in straightway with haste unto the king, and asked, saying, I will that thou forthwith give me in a charger the
26 head of John [5] the Baptist. And the king was exceeding sorry; but for the sake of his oaths, and of them that sat
27 at meat, he would not reject her. And straightway the king sent forth a soldier of his guard, and commanded to bring his head: and he went and be-
28 headed him in the prison, and brought his head in a charger, and gave it to the damsel; and the damsel gave it to
29 her mother. And when his disciples heard *thereof*, they came and took up his corpse, and laid it in a tomb.
30 And the apostles gather themselves together unto Jesus; and they told him all things, whatsoever they had done,
31 and whatsoever they had taught. And he saith unto them, Come ye yourselves apart into a desert place, and rest a while. For there were many coming and going, and they had no
32 leisure so much as to eat. And they went away in the boat to a desert place
33 apart. And *the people* saw them going, and many knew *them*, and they ran there together [6] on foot from all the
34 cities, and outwent them. And he came forth and saw a great multitude, and he had compassion on them, because they were as sheep not having a shepherd: and he began to teach them
35 many things. And when the day was now far spent, his disciples came unto

---

1 Many ancient authorities read *did many things*.
2 Or, *military tribunes* Gr. *chiliarchs*.
3 Some ancient authorities read *his daughter Herodias*.
4 Or, *it*
5 Gr. *the Baptizer*.
6 Or, *by land*

K. James Vers.

against him, and would have killed him; but she could not:
20 For Herod feared John, knowing that he was a just man and a holy, and observed him; and when he heard him, he did many things, and heard him gladly.
21 And when a convenient day was come, that Herod on his birthday made a supper to his lords, high captains, and chief *estates* of Galilee;
22 And when the daughter of the said Herodias came in, and danced, and pleased Herod and them that sat with him, the king said unto the damsel, Ask of me whatsoever thou wilt, and I will give *it* thee.
23 And he sware unto her, Whatsoever thou shalt ask of me, I will give *it* thee, unto the half of my kingdom.
24 And she went forth, and said unto her mother, What shall I ask? And she said, The head of John the Baptist.
25 And she came in straightway with haste unto the king, and asked, saying, I will that thou give me by and by in a charger the head of John the Baptist.
26 And the king was exceeding sorry; *yet* for his oath's sake, and for their sakes which sat with him, he would not reject her.
27 And immediately the king sent an executioner, and commanded his head to be brought: and he went and beheaded him in the prison,
28 And brought his head in a charger, and gave it to the damsel; and the damsel gave it to her mother.
29 And when his disciples heard *of it*, they came and took up his corpse, and laid it in a tomb.
30 And the apostles gathered themselves together unto Jesus, and told him all things, both what they had done, and what they had taught.
31 And he said unto them, Come ye yourselves apart into a desert place, and rest awhile: for there were many coming and going, and they had no leisure so much as to eat.
32 And they departed into a desert place by ship privately.
33 And the people saw them departing, and many knew him, and ran afoot thither out of all cities, and outwent them, and came together unto him.
34 And Jesus, when he came out, saw much people, and was moved with compassion toward them, because they were as sheep not having a shepherd: and he began to teach them many things.
35 And when the day was now far spent, his disciples came unto him, and said,

20 desired to kill him; and she could not; for Herod feared John, knowing that he was a righteous man and a holy, and kept him safe. And when he heard him, he
21 ¹was much perplexed; and he heard him gladly. And when a convenient day was come, that Herod on his birthday made a supper to his lords, and the ²high
22 captains, and the chief men of Galilee; and when ³the daughter of Herodias herself came in and danced, ⁴she pleased Herod and them that sat at meat with him; and the king said unto the damsel, Ask of me whatsoever
23 thou wilt, and I will give it thee. And he sware unto her, Whatsoever thou shalt ask of me, I will give it thee,
24 unto the half of my kingdom. And she went out, and said unto her mother, What shall I ask? And she
25 said, The head of John ⁵the Baptist. And she came in straightway with haste unto the king, and asked, saying, I will that thou forthwith give me in a charger
26 the head of John ⁵the Baptist. And the king was exceeding sorry; but for the sake of his oaths, and of them that sat at meat, he would not reject her.
27 And straightway the king sent forth a soldier of his guard, and commanded to bring his head: and he
28 went and beheaded him in the prison, and brought his head in a charger, and gave it to the damsel; and the
29 damsel gave it to her mother. And when his disciples heard *thereof*, they came and took up his corpse, and laid it in a tomb.
30 And the apostles gather themselves together unto Jesus; and they told him all things, whatsoever they
31 had done, and whatsoever they had taught. And he saith unto them, Come ye yourselves apart into a desert place, and rest a while. For there were many coming and going, and they had no leisure so much as
32 to eat. And they went away in the boat to a desert
33 place apart. And *the people* saw them going, and many knew *them*, and they ran there together ⁶on foot
34 from all the cities, and outwent them. And he came forth and saw a great multitude, and he had compassion on them, because they were as sheep not having a shepherd: and he began to teach them many things.
35 And when the day was now far spent, his disciples

¹ Many ancient authorities read *did many things.*
² Or, *military tribunes* Gr. *chiliarchs.*
³ Some ancient authorities read *his daughter Herodias.*
⁴ Or, *it*
⁵ Gr. *the Baptizer.*

⁶ Or, *by land*

Eng. Revision	K. James Vers.
him, and said, The place is desert, and 36 the day is now far spent: send them away, that they may go into the country and villages round about, and buy 37 themselves somewhat to eat. But he answered and said unto them, Give ye them to eat. And they say unto him, Shall we go and buy two hundred [1] pennyworth of bread, and give them to 38 eat? And he saith unto them, How many loaves have ye? go and see. And when they knew, they say, Five, and 39 two fishes. And he commanded them that all should [2] sit down by companies 40 upon the green grass. And they sat down in ranks, by hundreds, and by 41 fifties. And he took the five loaves and the two fishes, and looking up to heaven, he blessed, and brake the loaves; and he gave to the disciples to set before them; and the two fishes divided 42 he among them all. And they did all 43 eat, and were filled. And they took up broken pieces, twelve basketfuls, and 44 also of the fishes. And they that ate the loaves were five thousand men. 45 And straightway he constrained his disciples to enter into the boat, and to go before *him* unto the other side to Bethsaida, while he himself sendeth 46 the multitude away. And after he had taken leave of them, he departed into 47 the mountain to pray. And when even was come, the boat was in the midst of 48 the sea, and he alone on the land. And seeing them distressed in rowing, for the wind was contrary unto them, about the fourth watch of the night he cometh unto them, walking on the sea; and he would have passed by them: 49 but they, when they saw him walking on the sea, supposed that it was an ap- 50 parition, and cried out: for they all saw him, and were troubled. But he straightway spake with them, and saith unto them, Be of good cheer: it 51 is I; be not afraid. And he went up unto them into the boat; and the wind ceased: and they were sore amazed in 52 themselves; for they understood not concerning the loaves, but their heart was hardened. 53 And when they had [3] crossed over, they came to the land unto Gennesaret, 54 and moored to the shore. And when they were come out of the boat,	This is a desert place, and now the time *is* far passed: 36 Send them away, that they may go into the country round about, and into the villages, and buy themselves bread: for they have nothing to eat. 37 He answered and said unto them, Give ye them to eat. And they say unto him, Shall we go and buy two hundred pennyworth of bread, and give them to eat? 38 He saith unto them, How many loaves have ye? go and see. And when they knew, they say, Five, and two fishes. 39 And he commanded them to make all sit down by companies upon the green grass. 40 And they sat down in ranks, by hundreds, and by fifties. 41 And when he had taken the five loaves and the two fishes, he looked up to heaven, and blessed, and brake the loaves, and gave *them* to his disciples to set before them; and the two fishes divided he among them all. 42 And they did all eat, and were filled. 43 And they took up twelve baskets full of the fragments, and of the fishes. 44 And they that did eat of the loaves were about five thousand men. 45 And straightway he constrained his disciples to get into the ship, and to go to the other side before unto Bethsaida, while he sent away the people. 46 And when he had sent them away, he departed into a mountain to pray. 47 And when even was come, the ship was in the midst of the sea, and he alone on the land. 48 And he saw them toiling in rowing; for the wind was contrary unto them: and about the fourth watch of the night he cometh unto them, walking upon the sea, and would have passed by them. 49 But when they saw him walking upon the sea, they supposed it had been a spirit, and cried out: 50 For they all saw him, and were troubled. And immediately he talked with them, and saith unto them, Be of good cheer: it is I; be not afraid. 51 And he went up unto them into the ship; and the wind ceased: and they were sore amazed in themselves beyond measure, and wondered. 52 For they considered not *the miracle* of the loaves; for their heart was hardened. 53 And when they had passed over, they came into the land of Gennesaret, and drew to the shore. 54 And when they were come out of the ship, straightway they knew him,

1 See marginal note on Matt. xviii. 28.
2 Gr. *recline*.
3 Or, *crossed over to the land, they came unto Gennesaret*

came unto him, and said, The place is desert, and the
36 day is now far spent: send them away, that they may
go into the country and villages round about, and buy
37 themselves somewhat to eat. But he answered and
said unto them, Give ye them to eat. And they say
unto him, Shall we go and buy two hundred ¹shillings'
38 worth of bread, and give them to eat? And he saith
unto them, How many loaves have ye? go *and* see.
And when they knew, they say, Five, and two fishes.
39 And he commanded them that all should ²sit down by
40 companies upon the green grass. And they sat down
41 in ranks, by hundreds, and by fifties. And he took
the five loaves and the two fishes, and looking up to
heaven, he blessed, and brake the loaves; and he
gave to the disciples to set before them; and the two
42 fishes divided he among them all. And they did all
43 eat, and were filled. And they took up broken pieces,
44 twelve basketfuls, and also of the fishes. And they
that ate the loaves were five thousand men.
45 And straightway he constrained his disciples to enter
into the boat, and to go before *him* unto the other side
to Bethsaida, while he himself sendeth the multitude
46 away. And after he had taken leave of them, he de-
47 parted into the mountain to pray. And when even
was come, the boat was in the midst of the sea, and
48 he alone on the land. And seeing them distressed in
rowing, for the wind was contrary unto them, about
the fourth watch of the night he cometh unto them,
walking on the sea; and he would have passed by
49 them: but they, when they saw him walking on the
sea, supposed that it was an apparition, and cried
50 out: for they all saw him, and were troubled. But
he straightway spake with them, and saith unto them,
51 Be of good cheer: it is I; be not afraid. And he
went up unto them into the boat; and the wind
52 ceased: and they were sore amazed in themselves; for
they understood not concerning the loaves, but their
heart was hardened.
53 And when they had ³crossed over, they came to the
54 land unto Gennesaret, and moored to the shore. And
when they were come out of the boat, straightway *the*

¹ See marginal note on Matt. xviii. 28.

² Gr. *recline.*

³ Or, *crossed over to the land, they came unto Gennesaret*

Eng. Revision.

55 straightway *the people* knew him, and ran round about that whole region, and began to carry about on their beds those that were sick, where they heard
56 he was. And wheresoever he entered, into villages, or into cities, or into the country, they laid the sick in the marketplaces, and besought him that they might touch if it were but the border of his garment: and as many as touched ¹ him were made whole.

7 And there are gathered together unto him the Pharisees, and certain of the scribes, which had come from Jerusa-
2 lem, and had seen that some of his disciples ate their bread with ² defiled,
3 that is, unwashen, hands. For the Pharisees, and all the Jews, except they wash their hands ³ diligently, eat not, holding the tradition of the elders;
4 and *when they come* from the marketplace, except they ⁴ wash themselves, they eat not: and many other things there be, which they have received to hold, ⁵ washings of cups, and pots, and
5 brasen vessels ⁶. And the Pharisees and the scribes ask him, Why walk not thy disciples according to the tradition of the elders, but eat their bread with
6 ² defiled hands? And he said unto them, Well did Isaiah prophesy of you hypocrites, as it is written,
This people honoureth me with their lips,
But their heart is far from me.
7 But in vain do they worship me,
Teaching *as their* doctrines the precepts of men.
8 Ye leave the commandment of God, and hold fast the tradition of men.
9 And he said unto them, Full well do ye reject the commandment of God, that
10 ye may keep your tradition. For Moses said, Honour thy father and thy mother; and, He that speaketh evil of father or mother, let him ⁷ die the death:
11 but ye say, If a man shall say to his father or his mother, That wherewith thou mightest have been profited by me is Corban, that is to say, Given *to*
12 *God*; ye no longer suffer him to do aught for his father or his mother;
13 making void the word of God by your tradition, which ye have delivered: and
14 many such like things ye do. And he called to him the multitude again, and said unto them, Hear me all of you,

1 Or, *it*
2 Or, *common*
3 Or, *up to the elbow* Gr. *with the fist.*
4 Gr. *baptize.* Some ancient authorities read *sprinkle themselves.*
5 Gr. *baptizings.*
6 Many ancient authorities add *and couches.*
7 Or, *surely die*

S. MARK.

K. James Vers.

55 And ran through that whole region round about, and began to carry about in beds those that were sick, where they heard he was.
56 And whithersoever he entered, into villages, or cities, or country, they laid the sick in the streets, and besought him that they might touch if it were but the border of his garment: and as many as touched him were made whole.

CHAPTER VII.

THEN came together unto him the Pharisees, and certain of the scribes, which came from Jerusalem.
2 And when they saw some of his disciples eat bread with defiled, that is to say, with unwashen hands, they found fault.
3 For the Pharisees, and all the Jews, except they wash *their* hands oft, eat not, holding the tradition of the elders.
4 And *when they come* from the market, except they wash, they eat not. And many other things there be, which they have received to hold, *as* the washing of cups, and pots, brazen vessels, and of tables.
5 Then the Pharisees and scribes asked him, Why walk not thy disciples according to the tradition of the elders, but eat bread with unwashen hands?
6 He answered and said unto them, Well hath Esaias prophesied of you hypocrites, as it is written, This people honoureth me with *their* lips, but their heart is far from me.
7 Howbeit in vain do they worship me, teaching *for* doctrines the commandments of men.
8 For laying aside the commandment of God, ye hold the tradition of men, *as* the washing of pots and cups: and many other such like things ye do.
9 And he said unto them, Full well ye reject the commandment of God, that ye may keep your own tradition.
10 For Moses said, Honour thy father and thy mother; and, Whoso curseth father or mother, let him die the death:
11 But ye say, If a man shall say to his father or mother, *It is* Corban, that is to say, a gift, by whatsoever thou mightest be profited by me; *he shall be free.*
12 And ye suffer him no more to do aught for his father or his mother;
13 Making the word of God of none effect through your tradition, which ye have delivered: and many such like things do ye.
14 ¶ And when he had called all the people *unto him*, he said unto them, Hearken unto me every one *of you*, and understand:

55 *people* knew him, and ran round about that whole region, and began to carry about on their ¹beds those
56 that were sick, where they heard he was. And wheresoever he entered, into villages, or into cities, or into the country, they laid the sick in the marketplaces, and besought him that they might touch if it were but the border of his garment: and as many as touched him were made whole.

7 And there are gathered together unto him the Pharisees, and certain of the scribes, that had come from
2 Jerusalem, and had seen that some of his disciples ate their bread with ³defiled, that is, unwashen, hands.
3 For the Pharisees, and all the Jews, except they wash their hands ⁴diligently, eat not, holding the tradition of
4 the elders: and *when they come* from the marketplace, except they ⁵bathe themselves, they eat not: and many other things there are, which they have received to hold, ⁶washings of cups, and pots, and brasen vessels⁷.
5 And the Pharisees and the scribes ask him, Why walk not thy disciples according to the tradition of the
6 elders, but eat their bread with ³defiled hands? And he said unto them, Well did Isaiah prophesy of you hypocrites, as it is written,

This people honoureth me with their lips,
But their heart is far from me.
7 But in vain do they worship me,
Teaching *as their* doctrines the precepts of men.

8 Ye leave the commandment of God, and hold fast the
9 tradition of men. And he said unto them, Full well do ye reject the commandment of God, that ye may
10 keep your tradition. For Moses said, Honour thy father and thy mother; and, He that speaketh evil of
11 father or mother, let him ⁸die the death: but ye say, If a man shall say to his father or his mother, That wherewith thou mightest have been profited by me is
12 Corban, that is to say, Given *to God*; ye no longer suffer him to do aught for his father or his mother;
13 making void the word of God by your tradition, which ye have delivered: and many such like things ye do.
14 And he called to him the multitude again, and said unto them, Hear me all of you, and understand:

¹ Or, *pallets*

² Or, *it*

³ Or, *common*

⁴ Or, *up to the elbow*
Gr. *with the fist.*
⁵ Gr. *baptize.*
Some ancient authorities read *sprinkle themselves.*
⁶ Gr. *baptizings.*
⁷ Many ancient authorities add *and couches.*

⁸ Or, *surely die*

Eng. Revision — S. MARK

15 and understand: there is nothing from without the man, that going into him can defile him: but the things which proceed out of the man are those that
17 defile the man.[1] And when he was entered into the house from the multitude, his disciples asked of him the
18 parable. And he saith unto them, Are ye so without understanding also? Perceive ye not, that whatsoever from without goeth into the man, it cannot
19 defile him; because it goeth not into his heart, but into his belly, and goeth out into the draught? *This he said,*
20 *making all meats clean.* And he said, That which proceedeth out of the man,
21 that defileth the man. For from within, out of the heart of men, [2] evil thoughts
22 proceed, fornications, thefts, murders, adulteries, covetings, wickednesses, deceit, lasciviousness, an evil eye, rail-
23 ing, pride, foolishness: all these evil things proceed from within, and defile the man.
24 And from thence he arose, and went away into the borders of Tyre [3] and Sidon. And he entered into a house, and would have no man know it: and he
25 could not be hid. But straightway a woman, whose little daughter had an unclean spirit, having heard of him,
26 came and fell down at his feet. Now the woman was a [4] Greek, a Syrophœnician by race. And she besought him that he would cast forth the [5] devil out
27 of her daughter. And he said unto her, Let the children first be filled: for it is not meet to take the children's [6] bread
28 and cast it to the dogs. But she answered and saith unto him, Yea, Lord: even the dogs under the table eat of the
29 children's crumbs. And he said unto her, For this saying go thy way; the [5] devil is gone out of thy daughter.
30 And she went away unto her house, and found the child laid upon the bed, and the [5] devil gone out.
31 And again he went out from the borders of Tyre, and came through Sidon unto the sea of Galilee, through the
32 midst of the borders of Decapolis. And they bring unto him one that was deaf, and had an impediment in his speech; and they beseech him to lay his hand
33 upon him. And he took him aside from the multitude privately, and put his fin-

[1] Many ancient authorities insert ver. 16 *If any man hath ears to hear, let him hear.*
[2] Gr. *thoughts that are evil.*
[3] Some ancient authorities omit *and Sidon.*
[4] Or, *Gentile*
[5] Gr. *demon.*
[6] Or, *loaf*

K. James Vers. — S. MARK

15 There is nothing from without a man, that entering into him can defile him: but the things which come out of him, those are they that defile the man.
16 If any man have ears to hear, let him hear.
17 And when he was entered into the house from the people, his disciples asked him concerning the parable.
18 And he saith unto them, Are ye so without understanding also? Do ye not perceive, that whatsoever thing from without entereth into the man, it cannot defile him;
19 Because it entereth not into his heart, but into the belly, and goeth out into the draught, purging all meats?
20 And he said, That which cometh out of the man, that defileth the man.
21 For from within, out of the heart of men, proceed evil thoughts, adulteries, fornications, murders,
22 Thefts, covetousness, wickedness, deceit, lasciviousness, an evil eye, blasphemy, pride, foolishness:
23 All these evil things come from within, and defile the man.
24 ¶ And from thence he arose, and went into the borders of Tyre and Sidon, and entered into a house, and would have no man know *it:* but he could not be hid.
25 For a *certain* woman, whose young daughter had an unclean spirit, heard of him, and came and fell at his feet:
26 The woman was a Greek, a Syrophenician by nation; and she besought him that he would cast forth the devil out of her daughter.
27 But Jesus said unto her, Let the children first be filled: for it is not meet to take the children's bread, and to cast *it* unto the dogs.
28 And she answered and said unto him, Yes, Lord: yet the dogs under the table eat of the children's crumbs.
29 And he said unto her, For this saying go thy way; the devil is gone out of thy daughter.
30 And when she was come to her house, she found the devil gone out, and her daughter laid upon the bed.
31 ¶ And again, departing from the coasts of Tyre and Sidon, he came unto the sea of Galilee, through the midst of the coasts of Decapolis.
32 And they bring unto him one that was deaf, and had an impediment in his speech; and they beseech him to put his hand upon him.
33 And he took him aside from the multitude, and put his fingers into his ears, and he spit, and touched his tongue;

15 there is nothing from without the man, that going into him can defile him: but the things which proceed out
17 of the man are those that defile the man.[1] And when
18 he was entered into the house from the multitude, his disciples asked of him the parable. And he saith unto them, Are ye so without understanding also? Perceive ye not, that whatsoever from without goeth into
19 the man, *it* cannot defile him; because it goeth not into his heart, but into his belly, and goeth out into the draught? *This he said,* making all meats clean.
20 And he said, That which proceedeth out of the man,
21 that defileth the man. For from within, out of the heart of men, [2] evil thoughts proceed, fornications,
22 thefts, murders, adulteries, covetings, wickednesses, deceit, lasciviousness, an evil eye, railing, pride, fool-
23 ishness: all these evil things proceed from within, and defile the man.
24 And from thence he arose, and went away into the borders of Tyre [3] and Sidon. And he entered into a house, and would have no man know it: and he could
25 not be hid. But straightway a woman, whose little daughter had an unclean spirit, having heard of him,
26 came and fell down at his feet. Now the woman was a [4] Greek, a Syrophœnician by race. And she besought him that he would cast forth the demon out of her daughter.
27 And he said unto her, Let the children first be filled: for it is not meet to take the children's [5] bread and
28 cast it to the dogs. But she answered and saith unto him, Yea, Lord: even the dogs under the table eat of
29 the children's crumbs. And he said unto her, For this saying go thy way; the demon is gone out of thy
30 daughter. And she went away unto her house, and found the child laid upon the bed, and the demon gone out.
31 And again he went out from the borders of Tyre, and came through Sidon unto the sea of Galilee,
32 through the midst of the borders of Decapolis. And they bring unto him one that was deaf, and had an impediment in his speech; and they beseech him to
33 lay his hand upon him. And he took him aside from the multitude privately, and put his fingers into his

[1] Many ancient authorities insert ver. 16 *If any man hath ears to hear, let him hear.*

[2] Gr. *thoughts that are evil.*

[3] Some ancient authorities omit *and Sidon.*

[4] Or, *Gentile*

[5] Or, *loaf*

Eng. Revision.

gers into his ears, and he spat, and
34 touched his tongue; and looking up to
heaven, he sighed, and saith unto him,
35 Ephphatha, that is, Be opened. And
his ears were opened, and the bond of
his tongue was loosed, and he spake
36 plain. And he charged them that they
should tell no man: but the more he
charged them, so much the more a great
37 deal they published it. And they were
beyond measure astonished, saying, He
hath done all things well: he maketh
even the deaf to hear, and the dumb
to speak.

8 In those days, when there was again
a great multitude, and they had nothing to eat, he called unto him his disci-
2 ples, and saith unto them, I have compassion on the multitude, because they
continue with me now three days, and
3 have nothing to eat: and if I send them
away fasting to their home, they will
faint in the way; and some of them are
4 come from far. And his disciples answered him, Whence shall one be able
to fill these men with [1] bread here in a
5 desert place? And he asked them, How
many loaves have ye? And they said,
6 Seven. And he commandeth the multitude to sit down on the ground: and
he took the seven loaves, and having
given thanks, he brake, and gave to his
disciples, to set before them; and they
7 set them before the multitude. And
they had a few small fishes: and having blessed them, he commanded to set
8 these also before them. And they did
eat, and were filled: and they took up,
of broken pieces that remained over,
9 seven baskets. And they were about
four thousand: and he sent them away.
10 And straightway he entered into the
boat with his disciples, and came into
the parts of Dalmanutha.
11 And the Pharisees came forth, and
began to question with him, seeking of
him a sign from heaven, tempting him.
12 And he sighed deeply in his spirit, and
saith, Why doth this generation seek a
sign? verily I say unto you, There shall
no sign be given unto this generation.
13 And he left them, and again entering
into *the boat* departed to the other side.
14 And they forgot to take bread; and
they had not in the boat with them
15 more than one loaf. And he charged
them, saying, Take heed, beware of the

---

[1] Gr. *loaves.*

S. MARK.   K. James Vers. 7. 33—

34 And looking up to heaven, he sighed,
and saith unto him, Ephphatha, that is,
Be opened.
35 And straightway his ears were
opened, and the string of his tongue was
loosed, and he spake plain.
36 And he charged them that they should
tell no man: but the more he charged
them, so much the more a great deal they
published *it;*
37 And were beyond measure astonished, saying, He hath done all things well:
he maketh both the deaf to hear, and the
dumb to speak.

CHAPTER VIII.

IN those days the multitude being very
great, and having nothing to eat, Jesus
called his disciples *unto him,* and saith
unto them,
2 I have compassion on the multitude,
because they have now been with me
three days, and have nothing to eat:
3 And if I send them away fasting to
their own houses, they will faint by the
way: for divers of them came from far.
4 And his disciples answered him, From
whence can a man satisfy these *men* with
bread here in the wilderness?
5 And he asked them, How many loaves
have ye? And they said, Seven.
6 And he commanded the people to sit
down on the ground: and he took the
seven loaves, and gave thanks, and brake,
and gave to his disciples to set before
them; and they did set *them* before the
people.
7 And they had a few small fishes: and
he blessed, and commanded to set them
also before *them.*
8 So they did eat, and were filled: and
they took up of the broken *meat* that was
left seven baskets.
9 And they that had eaten were about
four thousand: and he sent them away.
10 ¶ And straightway he entered into a
ship with his disciples, and came into the
parts of Dalmanutha.
11 And the Pharisees came forth, and
began to question with him, seeking of
him a sign from heaven, tempting him.
12 And he sighed deeply in his spirit, and
saith, Why doth this generation seek after
a sign? verily I say unto you, There shall
no sign be given unto this generation.
13 And he left them, and entering into
the ship again departed to the other side.
14 ¶ Now *the disciples* had forgotten to
take bread, neither had they in the ship
with them more than one loaf.
15 And he charged them, saying, Take
heed, beware of the leaven of the Pharisees, and *of* the leaven of Herod.

34 ears, and he spat, and touched his tongue; and looking up to heaven, he sighed, and saith unto him, Eph-
35 phatha, that is, Be opened. And his ears were opened, and the bond of his tongue was loosed, and he spake
36 plain. And he charged them that they should tell no man: but the more he charged them, so much the
37 more a great deal they published it. And they were beyond measure astonished, saying, He hath done all things well: he maketh even the deaf to hear, and the dumb to speak.

8 In those days, when there was again a great multitude, and they had nothing to eat, he called unto him
2 his disciples, and saith unto them, I have compassion on the multitude, because they continue with me now
3 three days, and have nothing to eat: and if I send them away fasting to their home, they will faint in the
4 way; and some of them are come from far. And his disciples answered him, Whence shall one be able to fill these men with ¹bread here in a desert place? ¹ Gr. *loaves.*
5 And he asked them, How many loaves have ye? And
6 they said, Seven. And he commandeth the multitude to sit down on the ground: and he took the seven loaves, and having given thanks, he brake, and gave to his disciples, to set before them; and they set them before the
7 multitude. And they had a few small fishes: and having blessed them, he commanded to set these also before
8 them. And they did eat, and were filled: and they took up, of broken pieces that remained over, seven baskets.
9 And they were about four thousand: and he sent them
10 away. And straightway he entered into the boat with his disciples, and came into the parts of Dalmanutha.
11 And the Pharisees came forth, and began to question with him, seeking of him a sign from heaven,
12 trying him. And he sighed deeply in his spirit, and saith, Why doth this generation seek a sign? verily I say unto you, There shall no sign be given
13 unto this generation. And he left them, and again entering into *the boat* departed to the other side.
14 And they forgot to take bread; and they had not in
15 the boat with them more than one loaf. And he charged them, saying, Take heed, beware of the leaven

Eng. Revision.

leaven of the Pharisees and the leaven
16 of Herod. And they reasoned one with
another, ¹ saying, ² We have no bread.
17 And Jesus perceiving it saith unto them,
Why reason ye, because ye have no
bread? do ye not yet perceive, neither
understand? have ye your heart hard-
18 ened? Having eyes, see ye not? and
having ears, hear ye not? and do ye
19 not remember? When I brake the five
loaves among the five thousand, how
many ³ baskets full of broken pieces
took ye up? They say unto him, Twelve.
20 And when the seven among the four
thousand, how many ³ basketfuls of
broken pieces took ye up? And they
21 say unto him, Seven. And he said unto
them, Do ye not yet understand?
22 And they come unto Bethsaida. And
they bring to him a blind man, and be-
23 seech him to touch him. And he took
hold of the blind man by the hand, and
brought him out of the village; and
when he had spit on his eyes, and laid
his hands upon him, he asked him,
24 Seest thou aught? And he looked up,
and said, I see men; for I behold them
25 as trees, walking. Then again he laid
his hands upon his eyes; and he looked
stedfastly, and was restored, and saw
26 all things clearly. And he sent him
away to his home, saying, Do not even
enter into the village.
27 And Jesus went forth, and his disciples, into the villages of Cæsarea Philippi: and in the way he asked his disciples, saying unto them, Who do men
28 say that I am? And they told him, saying, John the Baptist: and others, Elijah: but others, One of the prophets.
29 And he asked them, But who say ye
that I am? Peter answereth and saith
30 unto him, Thou art the Christ. And he
charged them that they should tell no
31 man of him. And he began to teach
them, that the Son of man must suffer
many things, and be rejected by the
elders, and the chief priests, and the
scribes, and be killed, and after three
32 days rise again. And he spake the saying openly. And Peter took him, and
33 began to rebuke him. But he turning
about, and seeing his disciples, rebuked
Peter, and saith, Get thee behind me,
Satan: for thou mindest not the things

---

1 Some ancient authorities read *because they had no bread*.
2 Or, *It is because we have no bread*
3 *Basket* in ver. 19 and 20 represents different Greek words.

K. James Vers.

16 And they reasoned among themselves, saying, *It is* because we have no
bread.
17 And when Jesus knew *it*, he saith
unto them, Why reason ye, because ye
have no bread? perceive ye not yet,
neither understand? have ye your heart
yet hardened?
18 Having eyes, see ye not? and having
ears, hear ye not? and do ye not remember?
19 When I brake the five loaves among
five thousand, how many baskets full of
fragments took ye up? They say unto
him, Twelve.
20 And when the seven among four
thousand, how many baskets full of fragments took ye up? And they said, Seven.
21 And he said unto them, How is it that
ye do not understand?
22 ¶ And he cometh to Bethsaida; and
they bring a blind man unto him, and besought him to touch him.
23 And he took the blind man by the
hand, and led him out of the town; and
when he had spit on his eyes, and put his
hands upon him, he asked him if he saw
aught.
24 And he looked up, and said, I see
men as trees, walking.
25 After that he put *his* hands again
upon his eyes, and made him look up;
and he was restored, and saw every man
clearly.
26 And he sent him away to his house,
saying, Neither go into the town, nor tell
it to any in the town.
27 ¶ And Jesus went out, and his disciples, into the towns of Cesarea Philippi:
and by the way he asked his disciples,
saying unto them, Whom do men say that
I am?
28 And they answered, John the Baptist: but some *say*, Elias; and others, One
of the prophets.
29 And he saith unto them, But whom
say ye that I am? And Peter answereth
and saith unto him, Thou art the Christ.
30 And he charged them that they
should tell no man of him.
31 And he began to teach them, that
the Son of man must suffer many things,
and be rejected of the elders, and *of* the
chief priests, and scribes, and be killed,
and after three days rise again.
32 And he spake that saying openly.
And Peter took him, and began to rebuke
him.
33 But when he had turned about and
looked on his disciples, he rebuked Peter,
saying, Get thee behind me, Satan: for
thou savourest not the things that be of
God, but the things that be of men.

16 of the Pharisees and the leaven of Herod. And they
17 reasoned one with another, ¹ saying, ² We have no
bread. And Jesus perceiving it saith unto them,
Why reason ye, because ye have no bread? do ye not
yet perceive, neither understand? have ye your heart
18 hardened? Having eyes, see ye not? and having
19 ears, hear ye not? and do ye not remember? When
I brake the five loaves among the five thousand,
how many ³ baskets full of broken pieces took ye up?
20 They say unto him, Twelve. And when the seven
among the four thousand, how many ³ basketfuls of
21 broken pieces took ye up? And they say unto him,
Seven. And he said unto them, Do ye not yet understand?

22 And they come unto Bethsaida. And they bring to
23 him a blind man, and beseech him to touch him. And
he took hold of the blind man by the hand, and
brought him out of the village; and when he had spit
on his eyes, and laid his hands upon him, he asked
24 him, Seest thou aught? And he looked up, and said,
25 I see men; for I behold *them* as trees, walking. Then
again he laid his hands upon his eyes; and he looked
stedfastly, and was restored, and saw all things
26 clearly. And he sent him away to his home, saying,
Do not even enter into the village.

27 And Jesus went forth, and his disciples, into the
villages of Cæsarea Philippi: and in the way he asked
his disciples, saying unto them, Who do men say that
28 I am? And they told him, saying, John the Baptist:
and others, Elijah; but others, One of the prophets.
29 And he asked them, But who say ye that I am? Peter
answereth and saith unto him, Thou art the Christ.
30 And he charged them that they should tell no man of
31 him. And he began to teach them, that the Son of
man must suffer many things, and be rejected by the
elders, and the chief priests, and the scribes, and be
32 killed, and after three days rise again. And he spake
the saying openly. And Peter took him, and began
33 to rebuke him. But he turning about, and seeing his
disciples, rebuked Peter, and saith, Get thee behind
me, Satan: for thou mindest not the things of God,

¹ Some ancient authorities read *because they had no bread.*

² Or, It is *because we have no bread*

³ *Basket* in ver. 19 and 20 represents different Greek words.

Eng. Revision.

34 of God, but the things of men. And he called unto him the multitude with his disciples, and said unto them, If any man would come after me, let him deny himself, and take up his cross, and fol-
35 low me. For whosoever would save his ¹life shall lose it; and whosoever shall lose his ¹life for my sake and the gos-
36 pel's shall save it. For what doth it profit a man, to gain the whole world,
37 and forfeit his ¹life? For what should a man give in exchange for his ¹life?
38 For whosoever shall be ashamed of me and of my words in this adulterous and sinful generation, the Son of man also shall be ashamed of him, when he cometh in the glory of his Father with the
9 holy angels. And he said unto them, Verily I say unto you, There be some here of them that stand by, which shall in no wise taste of death, till they see the kingdom of God come with power.
2 And after six days Jesus taketh with him Peter, and James, and John, and bringeth them up into a high mountain apart by themselves: and he was trans-
3 figured before them: and his garments became glistering, exceeding white; so as no fuller on earth can whiten them.
4 And there appeared unto them Elijah with Moses: and they were talking
5 with Jesus. And Peter answereth and saith to Jesus, Rabbi, it is good for us to be here: and let us make three ²tabernacles; one for thee, and one for Moses,
6 and one for Elijah. For he wist not what to answer; for they became sore
7 afraid. And there came a cloud overshadowing them: and there came a voice out of the cloud, This is my be
8 loved Son: hear ye him. And suddenly looking round about, they saw no one any more, save Jesus only with themselves.
9 And as they were coming down from the mountain, he charged them that they should tell no man what things they had seen, save when the Son of man should have risen again from the
10 dead. And they kept the saying, questioning among themselves what the rising again from the dead should mean.
11 And they asked him, saying, ³The scribes say that Elijah must first come.
12 And he said unto them, Elijah indeed cometh first, and restoreth all things:

---
1 Or, *soul*
2 Or, *booths*
3 Or, How is it *that the scribes say . . . come?*

S. MARK. K. James Vers.

34 ¶ And when he had called the people *unto him* with his disciples also, he said unto them, Whosoever will come after me, let him deny himself, and take up his cross, and follow me.
35 For whosoever will save his life shall lose it; but whosoever shall lose his life for my sake and the gospel's, the same shall save it.
36 For what shall it profit a man, if he shall gain the whole world, and lose his own soul?
37 Or what shall a man give in exchange for his soul?
38 Whosoever therefore shall be ashamed of me and of my words, in this adulterous and sinful generation, of him also shall the Son of man be ashamed, when he cometh in the glory of his Father with the holy angels.

CHAPTER IX.

AND he said unto them, Verily I say unto you, That there be some of them that stand here, which shall not taste of death, till they have seen the kingdom of God come with power.
2 ¶ And after six days Jesus taketh *with him* Peter, and James, and John, and leadeth them up into a high mountain apart by themselves: and he was transfigured before them.
3 And his raiment became shining, exceeding white as snow; so as no fuller on earth can white them.
4 And there appeared unto them Elias with Moses: and they were talking with Jesus.
5 And Peter answered and said to Jesus, Master, it is good for us to be here: and let us make three tabernacles; one for thee, and one for Moses, and one for Elias.
6 For he wist not what to say; for they were sore afraid.
7 And there was a cloud that overshadowed them: and a voice came out of the cloud, saying, This is my beloved Son: hear him.
8 And suddenly, when they had looked round about, they saw no man any more, save Jesus only with themselves.
9 And as they came down from the mountain, he charged them that they should tell no man what things they had seen, till the Son of man were risen from the dead.
10 And they kept that saying with themselves, questioning one with another what the rising from the dead should mean.
11 ¶ And they asked him, saying, Why say the scribes that Elias must first come?
12 And he answered and told them, Elias verily cometh first, and restoreth all

34 but the things of men. And he called unto him the multitude with his disciples, and said unto them, If any man would come after me, let him deny himself, 35 and take up his cross, and follow me. For whosoever would save his life shall lose it; and whosoever shall lose his life for my sake and the gospel's shall save 36 it. For what doth it profit a man, to gain the whole 37 world, and forfeit his [1]life? For what should a man 38 give in exchange for his [1]life? For whosoever shall be ashamed of me and of my words in this adulterous and sinful generation, the Son of man also shall be ashamed of him, when he cometh in the glory of his 9 Father with the holy angels. And he said unto them, Verily I say unto you, There are some here of them that stand *by*, who shall in no wise taste of death, till they see the kingdom of God come with power.

2 And after six days Jesus taketh with him Peter, and James, and John, and bringeth them up into a high mountain apart by themselves: and he was trans-3 figured before them: and his garments became glistering, exceeding white; so as no fuller on earth can 4 whiten them. And there appeared unto them Elijah 5 with Moses: and they were talking with Jesus. And Peter answereth and saith to Jesus, Rabbi, it is good for us to be here: and let us make three [2]tabernacles; one for thee, and one for Moses, and one for Elijah. 6 For he knew not what to answer; for they became sore 7 afraid. And there came a cloud overshadowing them: and there came a voice out of the cloud, This is my 8 beloved Son: hear ye him. And suddenly looking round about, they saw no one any more, save Jesus only with themselves.

9 And as they were coming down from the mountain, he charged them that they should tell no man what things they had seen, save when the Son of man should 10 have risen again from the dead. And they kept the saying, questioning among themselves what the rising 11 again from the dead should mean. And they asked him, saying, [3]The scribes say that Elijah must first come. 12 And he said unto them, Elijah indeed cometh first, and restoreth all things: and how is it written of the

[1] Or, *soul*
[2] Or, *booths*
[3] Or, How is it *that the scribes say... come?*

Eng. Revision.

and how is it written of the Son of man, that he should suffer many things and
13 be set at nought? But I say unto you, that Elijah is come, and they have also done unto him whatsoever they listed, even as it is written of him.
14 And when they came to the disciples, they saw a great multitude about them, and scribes questioning
15 with them. And straightway all the multitude, when they saw him, were greatly amazed, and running to him
16 saluted him. And he asked them,
17 What question ye with them? And one of the multitude answered him, ¹ Master, I brought unto thee my son,
18 which hath a dumb spirit; and wheresoever it taketh him, it ² dasheth him down: and he foameth, and grindeth his teeth, and pineth away: and I spake to thy disciples that they should cast it out; and they were not
19 able. And he answereth them and saith, O faithless generation, how long shall I be with you? how long shall I bear with you? bring him
20 unto me. And they brought him unto him: and when he saw him, straightway the spirit ³ tare him grievously; and he fell on the ground, and wal-
21 lowed foaming. And he asked his father, How long time is it since this hath come unto him? And he said,
22 From a child. And oft-times it hath cast him both into the fire and into the waters, to destroy him: but if thou canst do anything, have com-
23 passion on us, and help us. And Jesus said unto him, If thou canst! All things are possible to him that
24 believeth. Straightway the father of the child cried out, and said ⁴, I believe; help thou mine unbelief.
25 And when Jesus saw that a multitude came running together, he rebuked the unclean spirit, saying unto him, Thou dumb and deaf spirit, I command thee, come out of him, and enter no more into him.
26 And having cried out, and ⁵ torn him much, he came out: and the child became as one dead; insomuch that
27 the more part said, He is dead. But Jesus took him by the hand, and
28 raised him up; and he arose. And when he was come into the house, his disciples asked him privately, ⁵ saying, We could not cast it out.
29 And he said unto them, This kind can come out by nothing, save by prayer ⁶.

1 Or, Teacher
2 Or, rendeth him   3 Or, convulsed
4 Many ancient authorities add with tears.
5 Or, How is it that we could not cast it out?
6 Many ancient authorities add and fasting.

S. MARK.   K. James Vers. 9. 12—

things; and how it is written of the Son of man, that he must suffer many things, and be set at nought.
13 But I say unto you, That Elias is indeed come, and they have done unto him whatsoever they listed, as it is written of him.
14 ¶ And when he came to his disciples, he saw a great multitude about them, and the scribes questioning with them.
15 And straightway all the people, when they beheld him, were greatly amazed, and running to him saluted him.
16 And he asked the scribes, What question ye with them?
17 And one of the multitude answered and said, Master, I have brought unto thee my son, which hath a dumb spirit;
18 And wheresoever he taketh him, he teareth him; and he foameth, and gnasheth with his teeth, and pineth away: and I spake to thy disciples that they should cast him out; and they could not.
19 He answereth him, and saith, O faithless generation, how long shall I be with you? how long shall I suffer you? bring him unto me.
20 And they brought him unto him: and when he saw him, straightway the spirit tare him; and he fell on the ground, and wallowed foaming.
21 And he asked his father, How long is it ago since this came unto him? And he said, Of a child.
22 And ofttimes it hath cast him into the fire, and into the waters, to destroy him: but if thou canst do any thing, have compassion on us, and help us.
23 Jesus said unto him, If thou canst believe, all things are possible to him that believeth.
24 And straightway the father of the child cried out, and said with tears, Lord, I believe; help thou mine unbelief.
25 When Jesus saw that the people came running together, he rebuked the foul spirit, saying unto him, Thou dumb and deaf spirit, I charge thee, come out of him, and enter no more into him.
26 And the spirit cried, and rent him sore, and came out of him: and he was as one dead; insomuch that many said, He is dead.
27 But Jesus took him by the hand, and lifted him up; and he arose.
28 And when he was come into the house, his disciples asked him privately, Why could not we cast him out?
29 And he said unto them, This kind can come forth by nothing, but by prayer and fasting.

Son of man, that he should suffer many things and be
13 set at nought? But I say unto you, that Elijah is
come, and they have also done unto him whatsoever
they listed, even as it is written of him.
14 And when they came to the disciples, they saw a
great multitude about them, and scribes questioning
15 with them. And straightway all the multitude, when
they saw him, were greatly amazed, and running to
16 him saluted him. And he asked them, What question
17 ye with them? And one of the multitude answered
him, ¹Master, I brought unto thee my son, who hath
18 a dumb spirit; and wheresoever it taketh him, it
²dasheth him down: and he foameth, and grindeth his
teeth, and pineth away: and I spake to thy disciples
that they should cast it out; and they were not able.
19 And he answereth them and saith, O faithless generation, how long shall I be with you? how long shall I
20 bear with you? bring him unto me. And they brought
him unto him: and when he saw him, straightway the
spirit ³tare him grievously; and he fell on the ground,
21 and wallowed foaming. And he asked his father,
How long time is it since this hath come unto him?
22 And he said, From a child. And oft-times it hath cast
him both into the fire and into the waters, to destroy
him: but if thou canst do anything, have compassion
23 on us, and help us. And Jesus said unto him, If
thou canst! All things are possible to him that be-
24 lieveth. Straightway the father of the child cried out,
25 and said⁴, I believe; help thou mine unbelief. And
when Jesus saw that a multitude came running together, he rebuked the unclean spirit, saying unto
him, Thou dumb and deaf spirit, I command thee,
26 come out of him, and enter no more into him. And
having cried out, and ⁵torn him much, he came out:
and *the child* became as one dead; insomuch that the
27 more part said, He is dead. But Jesus took him by
28 the hand, and raised him up; and he arose. And
when he was come into the house, his disciples asked
29 him privately, ⁵*saying*, We could not cast it out. And
he said unto them, This kind can come out by nothing,
save by prayer⁶.

¹ Or, *Teacher*

² Or, *rendeth him*

³ Or, *convulsed*

⁴ Many ancient authorities add *with tears.*

⁵ Or, How is it *that we could not cast it out?*

⁶ Many ancient authorities add *and fasting.*

Eng. Revision. S. MARK. K. James Vers. 9. 30—

30 And they went forth from thence, and passed through Galilee; and he would not that any man should know 31 it. For he taught his disciples, and said u..to them, The Son of man is delivered up into the hands of men, and they shall kill him; and when he is killed, after three days he shall 32 rise again. But they understood not the saying, and were afraid to ask him.
33 And they came to Capernaum: and when he was in the house he asked them, What were ye reasoning in the 34 way? But they held their peace: for they had disputed one with another in the way, who was the ¹ greatest.
35 And he sat down, and called the twelve; and he saith unto them, If any man would be first, he shall be 36 last of all, and minister of all. And he took a little child, and set him in the midst of them: and taking him 37 in his arms, he said unto them, Whosoever shall receive one of such little children in my name, receiveth me: and whosoever receiveth me, receiveth not me, but him that sent me.
38 John said unto him, ² Master, we saw one casting out ³ devils in thy name: and we forbade him, because 39 he followed not us. But Jesus said, Forbid him not: for there is no man which shall do a ⁴ mighty work in my name, and be able quickly to speak 40 evil of me. For he that is not against 41 us is for us. For whosoever shall give you a cup of water to drink, ⁵ because ye are Christ's, verily I say unto you, he shall in no wise lose his reward.
42 And whosoever shall cause one of these little ones that believe ⁶ on me to stumble, it were better for him if ⁷ a great millstone were hanged about his neck, and he were cast into the 43 sea. And if thy hand cause thee to stumble, cut it off: it is good for thee to enter into life maimed, rather than having thy two hands to go into ⁸ hell.
45 into the unquenchable fire.⁹ And if thy foot cause thee to stumble, cut it off: it is good for thee to enter into life halt, rather than having thy two 47 feet to be cast into ⁸ hell. And if thine eye cause thee to stumble, cast it out: it is good for thee to enter into the kingdom of God with one eye, rather than having two eyes to be 48 cast into ⁸ hell: where their worm dieth not, and the fire is not quench-

30 ⁌ And they departed thence, and passed through Galilee; and he would not that any man should know it.
31 For he taught his disciples, and said unto them, The Son of man is delivered into the hands of men, and they shall kill him; and after that he is killed, he shall rise the third day.
32 But they understood not that saying, and were afraid to ask him.
33 ⁌ And he came to Capernaum: and being in the house he asked them, What was it that ye disputed among yourselves by the way?
34 But they held their peace: for by the way they had disputed among themselves, who should be the greatest.
35 And he sat down, and called the twelve, and saith unto them, If any man desire to be first, the same shall be last of all, and servant of all.
36 And he took a child, and set him in the midst of them: and when he had taken him in his arms, he said unto them,
37 Whosoever shall receive one of such children in my name, receiveth me; and whosoever shall receive me, receiveth not me, but him that sent me.
38 ⁌ And John answered him, saying, Master, we saw one casting out devils in thy name, and he followeth not us: and we forbade him, because he followeth not us.
39 But Jesus said, Forbid him not: for there is no man which shall do a miracle in my name, that can lightly speak evil of me.
40 For he that is not against us is on our part.
41 For whosoever shall give you a cup of water to drink in my name, because ye belong to Christ, verily I say unto you, he shall not lose his reward.
42 And whosoever shall offend one of these little ones that believe in me, it is better for him that a millstone were hanged about his neck, and he were cast into the sea.
43 And if thy hand offend thee, cut it off: it is better for thee to enter into life maimed, than having two hands to go into hell, into the fire that never shall be quenched:
44 Where their worm dieth not, and the fire is not quenched.
45 And if thy foot offend thee, cut it off: it is better for thee to enter halt into life, than having two feet to be cast into hell, into the fire that never shall be quenched:
46 Where their worm dieth not, and the fire is not quenched.
47 And if thine eye offend thee, pluck it out: it is better for thee to enter into the kingdom of God with one eye, than having two eyes to be cast into hell fire:
48 Where their worm dieth not, and the fire is not quenched.

1 Gr. greater. 2 Or, Teacher 3 Gr. demons.
4 Gr. power. 5 Gr. in name that ye are.
6 Many ancient authorities omit on me.
7 Gr. a millstone turned by an ass.
8. Gr. Gehenna.
9 Ver. 44 and 46 (which are identical with ver. 48) are omitted by the best ancient authorities.

30 And they went forth from thence, and passed through Galilee; and he would not that any man should know
31 it. For he taught his disciples, and said unto them, The Son of man is delivered up into the hands of men, and they shall kill him; and when he is killed, after
32 three days he shall rise again. But they understood not the saying, and were afraid to ask him.
33 And they came to Capernaum: and when he was in the house he asked them, What were ye reasoning
34 in the way? But they held their peace: for they had disputed one with another in the way, who *was* the
35 ¹greatest. And he sat down, and called the twelve; and he saith unto them, If any man would be first, he
36 shall be last of all, and minister of all. And he took a little child, and set him in the midst of them: and
37 taking him in his arms, he said unto them, Whosoever shall receive one of such little children in my name, receiveth me: and whosoever receiveth me, receiveth not me, but him that sent me.
38 John said unto him, ²Master, we saw one casting out demons in thy name: and we forbade him, because
39 he followed not us. But Jesus said, Forbid him not: for there is no man who shall do a ³mighty work in
40 my name, and be able quickly to speak evil of me. For
41 he that is not against us is for us. For whosoever shall give you a cup of water to drink, ⁴because ye are Christ's, verily I say unto you, he shall in no wise lose
42 his reward. And whosoever shall cause one of these little ones that believe ⁵on me to stumble, it were better for him if ⁶a great millstone were hanged about
43 his neck, and he were cast into the sea. And if thy hand cause thee to stumble, cut it off: it is good for thee to enter into life maimed, rather than having thy two hands to go into ⁷hell, into the unquenchable
45 fire.⁸ And if thy foot cause thee to stumble, cut it off: it is good for thee to enter into life halt, rather than
47 having thy two feet to be cast into ⁷hell. And if thine eye cause thee to stumble, cast it out: it is good for thee to enter into the kingdom of God with one eye, rather than having two eyes to be cast into ⁷hell;
48 where their worm dieth not, and the fire is not

¹ Gr. *greater.*

² Or, *Teacher*

³ Gr. *power.*

⁴ Gr. *in name that ye are.*

⁵ Many ancient authorities omit *on me.*
⁶ Gr. *a millstone turned by an ass.*
⁷ Gr. *Gehenna.*
⁸ Ver. 44 and 46 (which are identical with ver. 48) are omitted by the best ancient authorities.

Eng. Revision.

49 ed. For every one shall be salted with
50 fire¹. Salt is good: but if the salt have lost its saltness, wherewith will ye season it? Have salt in yourselves, and be at peace one with another.
10 And he arose from thence, and cometh into the borders of Judæa and beyond Jordan: and multitudes come together unto him again; and, as he was wont, he taught them
2 again. And there came unto him Pharisees, and asked him, Is it lawful for a man to put away *his* wife?
3 tempting him. And he answered and said unto them, What did Moses com-
4 mand you? And they said, Moses suffered to write a bill of divorce-
5 ment, and to put her away. But Jesus said unto them, For your hardness of heart he wrote you this com-
6 mandment. But from the beginning of the creation, Male and female
7 made he them. For this cause shall a man leave his father and mother,
8 ² and shall cleave to his wife; and the twain shall become one flesh: so that they are no more twain, but
9 one flesh. What therefore God hath joined together, let not man put
10 asunder. And in the house the disciples asked him again of this mat-
11 ter. And he saith unto them, Whosoever shall put away his wife, and marry another, committeth adultery
12 against her: and if she herself shall put away her husband, and marry another, she committeth adultery.
13 ´And they brought unto him little children, that he should touch them:
14 and the disciples rebuked them. But when Jesus saw it, he was moved with indignation, and said unto them, Suffer the little children to come unto me; forbid them not: for of
15 such is the kingdom of God. Verily I say unto you, Whosoever shall not receive the kingdom of God as a little child, he shall in no wise enter there-
16 in. And he took them in his arms, and blessed them, laying his hands upon them.
17 And as he was going forth ³into the way, there ran one to him, and kneeled to him, and asked him, Good ⁴Master, what shall I do
18 that I may inherit eternal life? And Jesus said unto him, Why callest thou me good? none is good save one,
19 *even* God. Thou knowest the commandments, Do not kill, Do not com-

---

¹ Many ancient authorities add *and every sacrifice shall be salted with salt.* See Lev. ii. 13.
² Some ancient authorities omit *and shall cleave to his wife.*
³ Or, *on his way*
⁴ Or, *Teacher*

S. MARK. K. James Vers.

49 For every one shall be salted with fire, and every sacrifice shall be salted with salt.
50 Salt *is* good: but if the salt have lost his saltness, wherewith will ye season it? Have salt in yourselves, and have peace one with another.

CHAPTER X.

AND he arose from thence, and cometh into the coasts of Judea by the farther side of Jordan: and the people resort unto him again; and, as he was wont, he taught them again.
2 ¶ And the Pharisees came to him, and asked him, Is it lawful for a man to put away *his* wife? tempting him.
3 And he answered and said unto them, What did Moses command you?
4 And they said, Moses suffered to write a bill of divorcement, and to put her away.
5 And Jesus answered and said unto them, For the hardness of your heart he wrote you this precept.
6 But from the beginning of the creation God made them male and female.
7 For this cause shall a man leave his father and mother, and cleave to his wife;
8 And they twain shall be one flesh: so then they are no more twain, but one flesh.
9 What therefore God hath joined together, let not man put asunder.
10 And in the house his disciples asked him again of the same *matter*.
11 And he saith unto them, Whosoever shall put away his wife, and marry another, committeth adultery against her.
12 And if a woman shall put away her husband, and be married to another, she committeth adultery.
13 ¶ And they brought young children to him, that he should touch them; and *his* disciples rebuked those that brought them.
14 But when Jesus saw *it*, he was much displeased, and said unto them, Suffer the little children to come unto me, and forbid them not; for of such is the kingdom of God.
15 Verily I say unto you, Whosoever shall not receive the kingdom of God as a little child, he shall not enter therein.
16 And he took them up in his arms, put *his* hands upon them, and blessed them.
17 ¶ And when he was gone forth into the way, there came one running and kneeled to him, and asked him, Good Master, what shall I do that I may inherit eternal life?
18 And Jesus said unto him, Why callest thou me good? *there is* none good but one, *that is*, God.
19 Thou knowest the commandments,

49 quenched. For every one shall be salted with fire[1].
50 Salt is good: but if the salt have lost its saltness, wherewith will ye season it? Have salt in yourselves, and be at peace one with another.

10 And he arose from thence, and cometh into the borders of Judæa and beyond Jordan: and multitudes come together unto him again; and, as he was wont,
2 he taught them again. And there came unto him Pharisees, and asked him, Is it lawful for a man to
3 put away *his* wife? trying him. And he answered and said unto them, What did Moses command you?
4 And they said, Moses suffered to write a bill of divorce-
5 ment, and to put her away. But Jesus said unto them, For your hardness of heart he wrote you this com-
6 mandment. But from the beginning of the creation,
7 Male and female made he them. For this cause shall a man leave his father and mother, [2] and shall cleave
8 to his wife; and the twain shall become one flesh: so
9 that they are no more twain, but one flesh. What therefore God hath joined together, let not man put
10 asunder. And in the house the disciples asked him
11 again of this matter. And he saith unto them, Whosoever shall put away his wife, and marry another,
12 committeth adultery against her: and if she herself shall put away her husband, and marry another, she committeth adultery.

13 And they were bringing unto him little children, that he should touch them: and the disciples rebuked them.
14 But when Jesus saw it, he was moved with indignation, and said unto them, Suffer the little children to come unto me; forbid them not: for [3] to such belongeth the
15 kingdom of God. Verily I say unto you, Whosoever shall not receive the kingdom of God as a little child,
16 he shall in no wise enter therein. And he took them in his arms, and blessed them, laying his hands upon them.
17 And as he was going forth [4] into the way, there ran one to him, and kneeled to him, and asked him, Good [5] Master, what shall I do that I may inherit eternal
18 life? And Jesus said unto him, Why callest thou
19 me good? none is good save one, *even* God. Thou knowest the commandments, Do not kill, Do not

[1] Many ancient authorities add *and every sacrifice shall be salted with salt.* See Lev. ii. 13.

[2] Some ancient authorities omit *and shall cleave to his wife.*

[3] Or, *of such is*

[4] Or, *on his way*

[5] Or, *Teacher*

Eng. Revision. S. MARK. K. James Vers. 10. 19–

mit adultery, Do not steal, Do not bear false witness, Do not defraud, 20 Honour thy father and mother. And he said unto him, ¹Master, all these things have I observed from my 21 youth. And Jesus looking upon him loved him, and said unto him, One thing thou lackest: go, sell whatsoever thou hast, and give to the poor, and thou shalt have treasure in 22 heaven: and come, follow me. But his countenance fell at the saying, and he went away sorrowful: for he was one that had great possessions. 23 And Jesus looked round about, and saith unto his disciples, How hardly shall they that have riches enter into 24 the kingdom of God! And the disciples were amazed at his words. But Jesus answereth again, and saith unto them, Children, how hard is it ²for them that trust in riches to enter into 25 the kingdom of God! It is easier for a camel to go through a needle's eye, than for a rich man to enter into the 26 kingdom of God. And they were astonished exceedingly, saying ³unto 27 him, Then who can be saved? Jesus looking upon them saith, With men it is impossible, but not with God: for all things are possible with God. 28 Peter began to say unto him, Lo, we have left all, and have followed thee. 29 Jesus said, Verily I say unto you, There is no man that hath left house, or brethren, or sisters, or mother, or father, or children, or lands, for my 30 sake, and for the gospel's sake, but he shall receive a hundredfold now in this time, houses, and brethren, and sisters, and mothers, and children, and lands, with persecutions: and in 31 the ⁴world to come eternal life. But many *that are* first shall be last; and the last first. 32 And they were in the way, going up to Jerusalem; and Jesus was going before them: and they were amazed; ⁵and they that followed were afraid. And he took again the twelve, and began to tell them the things that 33 were to happen unto him, *saying*, Behold, we go up to Jerusalem: and the Son of man shall be delivered unto the chief priests and the scribes; and they shall condemn him to death, and shall deliver him unto the Gen- 34 tiles: and they shall mock him, and shall spit upon him, and shall scourge

Do not commit adultery, Do not kill, Do not steal, Do not bear false witness, Defraud not, Honour thy father and mothe 20 And he answered and said unto hi Master, all these have I observed fro my youth. 21 Then Jesus beholding him loved hi and said unto him, One thing thou lac est: go thy way, sell whatsoever th hast, and give to the poor, and thou sh have treasure in heaven: and come, ta up the cross, and follow me. 22 And he was sad at that saying, a went away grieved: for he had great p sessions. 23 ¶ And Jesus looked round about, a saith unto his disciples, How hardly sh they that have riches enter into the kir dom of God! 24 And the disciples were astonished his words. But Jesus answereth aga and saith unto them, Children, how ha is it for them that trust in riches to ent into the kingdom of God! 25 It is easier for a camel to go throu the eye of a needle, than for a rich m to enter into the kingdom of God. 26 And they were astonished out measure, saying among themselves, W then can be saved? 27 And Jesus looking upon them sai With men *it is* impossible, but not wi God: for with God all things are possib 28 ¶ Then Peter began to say unto hi Lo, we have left all, and have follow thee. 29 And Jesus answered and said, Ver I say unto you, There is no man that ha left house, or brethren, or sisters, father, or mother, or wife, or children, lands, for my sake, and the gospel's, 30 But he shall receive a hundredfc now in this time, houses, and brethren,a sisters, and mothers, and children, a lands, with persecutions; and in the wo to come eternal life. 31 But many *that are* first shall be la and the last first. 32 ¶ And they were in the way going to Jerusalem: and Jesus went befc them: and they were amazed; and they followed, they were afraid. And took again the twelve, and began to t them what things should happen ur him, 33 *Saying*, Behold, we go up to Jeru lem; and the Son of man shall be deliver unto the chief priests, and unto t scribes; and they shall condemn him death, and shall deliver him to the G tiles: 34 And they shall mock him, and sh scourge him, and shall spit upon him, a

1 Or, *Teacher*
2 Some ancient authorities omit *for them that trust in riches*.
3 Many ancient authorities read *among themselves*.
4 Or, *age*
5 Or, *but some as they followed were afraid*

commit adultery, Do not steal, Do not bear false witness, Do not defraud, Honour thy father and mother.
20 And he said unto him, ¹Master, all these things have I
21 observed from my youth. And Jesus looking upon him loved him, and said unto him, One thing thou lackest: go, sell whatsoever thou hast, and give to the poor, and thou shalt have treasure in heaven: and
22 come, follow me. But his countenance fell at the saying, and he went away sorrowful: for he was one that had great possessions.
23 And Jesus looked round about, and saith unto his disciples, How hardly shall they that have riches enter
24 into the kingdom of God! And the disciples were amazed at his words. But Jesus answereth again, and saith unto them, Children, how hard is it ²for them that trust in riches to enter into the kingdom of
25 God! It is easier for a camel to go through a needle's eye, than for a rich man to enter into the kingdom
26 of God. And they were astonished exceedingly, say-
27 ing ³unto him, Then who can be saved? Jesus looking upon them saith, With men it is impossible, but not with God: for all things are possible with God.
28 Peter began to say unto him, Lo, we have left all, and
29 have followed thee. Jesus said, Verily I say unto you, There is no man that hath left house, or brethren, or sisters, or mother, or father, or children, or lands, for
30 my sake, and for the gospel's sake, but he shall receive a hundredfold now in this time, houses, and brethren, and sisters, and mothers, and children, and lands, with persecutions; and in the ⁴world to come eternal
31 life. But many *that are* first shall be last; and the last first.
32 And they were in the way, going up to Jerusalem; and Jesus was going before them: and they were amazed; and they that followed were afraid. And he took again the twelve, and began to tell them the
33 things that were to happen unto him, *saying*, Behold, we go up to Jerusalem; and the Son of man shall be delivered unto the chief priests and the scribes; and they shall condemn him to death, and shall deliver
34 him unto the Gentiles: and they shall mock him, and

¹ Or, *Teacher*

² Some ancient authorities omit *for them that trust in riches.*

³ Many ancient authorities read *among themselves.*

⁴ Or, *age*

Eng. Revision. S. MARK. K. James Vers.

Eng. Revision

him, and shall kill him; and after three days he shall rise again.

35 And there come near unto him James and John, the sons of Zebedee, saying unto him, ¹Master, we would that thou shouldest do for us whatsoever we shall ask of thee.

36 And he said unto them, What would ye that I should do for you?

37 And they said unto him, Grant unto us that we may sit, one on thy right hand, and one on *thy* left hand, in thy glory.

38 But Jesus said unto them, Ye know not what ye ask. Are ye able to drink the cup that I drink? or to be baptized with the baptism that I am baptized with?

39 And they said unto him, We are able. And Jesus said unto them, The cup that I drink ye shall drink; and with the baptism that I am baptized withal shall ye be baptized:

40 but to sit on my right hand or on *my* left hand is not mine to give: but *it is for them* for whom it hath been prepared.

41 And when the ten heard it, they began to be moved with indignation concerning James and John.

42 And Jesus called them to him, and saith unto them, Ye know that they which are accounted to rule over the Gentiles lord it over them; and their great ones exercise authority over them. But it is not so among you: but whosoever would become great among you, shall

43 be your ²minister: and whosoever would be first among you, shall be

45 ³servant of all. For verily the Son of man came not to be ministered unto, but to minister, and to give his life a ransom for many.

46 And they come to Jericho: and as he went out from Jericho, with his disciples and a great multitude, the son of Timæus, Bartimæus, a blind beggar,

47 was sitting by the way side. And when he heard that it was Jesus of Nazareth, he began to cry out, and say, Jesus, thou son of David, have mercy on me.

48 And many rebuked him, that he should hold his peace: but he cried out the more a great deal, Thou son of David,

49 have mercy on me. And Jesus stood still, and said, Call ye him. And they call the blind man, saying unto him, Be of good cheer: rise, he calleth thee.

50 And he, casting away his garment,

---

1 Or, *Teacher*
2 Or, *servant*
3 Gr. *bondservant*.

K. James Vers. 10. 34—

shall kill him; and the third day he shall rise again.

35 ¶ And James and John, the sons of Zebedee, come unto him, saying, Master, we would that thou shouldest do for us whatsoever we shall desire.

36 And he said unto them, What would ye that I should do for you?

37 They said unto him, Grant unto us that we may sit, one on thy right hand, and the other on thy left hand, in thy glory.

38 But Jesus said unto them, Ye know not what ye ask: can ye drink of the cup that I drink of? and be baptized with the baptism that I am baptized with?

39 And they said unto him, We can. And Jesus said unto them, Ye shall indeed drink of the cup that I drink of; and with the baptism that I am baptized withal shall ye be baptized:

40 But to sit on my right hand and on my left hand is not mine to give; but *it shall be given to them* for whom it is prepared.

41 And when the ten heard *it*, they began to be much displeased with James and John.

42 But Jesus called them *to him*, and saith unto them, Ye know that they which are accounted to rule over the Gentiles exercise lordship over them; and their great ones exercise authority upon them.

43 But so shall it not be among you: but whosoever will be great among you, shall be your minister:

44 And whosoever of you will be the chiefest, shall be servant of all.

45 For even the Son of man came not to be ministered unto, but to minister, and to give his life a ransom for many.

46 ¶ And they came to Jericho: and as he went out of Jericho with his disciples and a great number of people, blind Bartimeus, the son of Timeus, sat by the highway side begging.

47 And when he heard that it was Jesus of Nazareth, he began to cry out, and say, Jesus, *thou* Son of David, have mercy on me.

48 And many charged him that he should hold his peace: but he cried the more a great deal, *Thou* Son of David, have mercy on me.

49 And Jesus stood still, and commanded him to be called. And they call the blind man, saying unto him, Be of good comfort, rise; he calleth thee.

50 And he, casting away his garment, rose, and came to Jesus.

shall spit upon him, and shall scourge him, and shall
kill him; and after three days he shall rise again.
35 And there come near unto him James and John,
the sons of Zebedee, saying unto him, ¹ Master, we   ¹ Or, *Teacher*
would that thou shouldest do for us whatsoever we
36 shall ask of thee. And he said unto them, What
37 would ye that I should do for you? And they said
unto him, Grant unto us that we may sit, one on thy
right hand, and one on *thy* left hand, in thy glory.
38 But Jesus said unto them, Ye know not what ye ask.
Are ye able to drink the cup that I drink? or to be
baptized with the baptism that I am baptized with?
39 And they said unto him, We are able. And Jesus
said unto them, The cup that I drink ye shall drink;
and with the baptism that I am baptized withal shall
40 ye be baptized: but to sit on my right hand or on *my*
left hand is not mine to give: but *it is for them* for
41 whom it hath been prepared. And when the ten
heard it, they began to be moved with indignation
42 concerning James and John. And Jesus called them
to him, and saith unto them, Ye know that they
who are accounted to rule over the Gentiles lord it
over them; and their great ones exercise authority
43 over them. But it is not so among you: but whosoever would become great among you, shall be your
44 ² minister: and whosoever would be first among you,   ² Or, *servant*
45 shall be ³ servant of all. For the Son of man also   ³ Gr.
came not to be ministered unto, but to minister, and   *bondservant.*
to give his life a ransom for many.
46 And they come to Jericho: and as he went out
from Jericho, with his disciples and a great multitude,
the son of Timæus, Bartimæus, a blind beggar, was
47 sitting by the way side. And when he heard that it
was Jesus of Nazareth, he began to cry out, and say,
48 Jesus, thou son of David, have mercy on me. And
many rebuked him, that he should hold his peace:
but he cried out the more a great deal, Thou son of
49 David, have mercy on me. And Jesus stood still, and
said, Call ye him. And they call the blind man, saying unto him, Be of good cheer: rise, he calleth thee.
50 And he, casting away his garment, sprang up, and

Eng. Revision.

51 sprang up, and came to Jesus. And Jesus answered him, and said, What wilt thou that I should do unto thee? And the blind man said unto him, ¹ Rab-
52 boni, that I may receive my sight. And Jesus said unto him, Go thy way; thy faith hath ² made thee whole. And straightway he received his sight, and followed him in the way.

11 And when they draw nigh unto Jerusalem, unto Bethphage and Bethany, at the mount of Olives, he sendeth two
2 of his disciples, and saith unto them, Go your way into the village that is over against you: and straightway as ye enter into it, ye shall find a colt tied, whereon no man ever yet sat; loose him,
3 and bring him. And if any one say unto you, Why do ye this? say ye, The Lord hath need of him; and straightway he ³ will send him ⁴ back hither.
4 And they went away, and found a colt tied at the door without in the open
5 street; and they loose him. And certain of them that stood there said unto them, What do ye, loosing the colt?
6 And they said unto them even as Jesus
7 had said: and they let them go. And they bring the colt unto Jesus, and cast on him their garments; and he sat
8 upon him. And many spread their garments upon the way; and others ⁵ branches, which they had cut from
9 the fields. And they that went before, and they that followed, cried, Hosanna; Blessed is he that cometh in the name
10 of the Lord: Blessed is the kingdom that cometh, *the kingdom* of our father David: Hosanna in the highest.
11 And he entered into Jerusalem, into the temple; and when he had looked round about upon all things, it being now eventide, he went out unto Bethany with the twelve.
12 And on the morrow, when they were come out from Bethany, he hungered.
13 And seeing a fig tree afar off having leaves, he came, if haply he might find anything thereon: and when he came to it, he found nothing but leaves; for
14 it was not the season of figs. And he answered and said unto it, No man eat fruit from thee henceforward for ever. And his disciples heard it.

---

1 See John xx. 16.
2 Or, *saved thee*
3 Gr. *sendeth.*
4 Or, *again*
5 Gr. *layers of leaves.*

K. James Vers.

51 And Jesus answered and said unto him, What wilt thou that I should do unto thee? The blind man said unto him, Lord, that I might receive my sight.
52 And Jesus said unto him, Go thy way; thy faith hath made thee whole. And immediately he received his sight, and followed Jesus in the way.

CHAPTER XI.

AND when they came nigh to Jerusalem, unto Bethphage and Bethany, at the mount of Olives, he sendeth forth two of his disciples,
2 And saith unto them, Go your way into the village over against you: and as soon as ye be entered into it, ye shall find a colt tied, whereon never man sat; loose him, and bring *him*.
3 And if any man say unto you, Why do ye this? say ye that the Lord hath need of him; and straightway he will send him hither.
4 And they went their way, and found the colt tied by the door without in a place where two ways met; and they loose him.
5 And certain of them that stood there said unto them, What do ye, loosing the colt?
6 And they said unto them even as Jesus had commanded: and they let them go.
7 And they brought the colt to Jesus, and cast their garments on him; and he sat upon him.
8 And many spread their garments in the way; and others cut down branches off the trees, and strewed *them* in the way.
9 And they that went before, and they that followed, cried, saying, Hosanna; Blessed is he that cometh in the name of the Lord:
10 Blessed be the kingdom of our father David, that cometh in the name of the Lord: Hosanna in the highest.
11 And Jesus entered into Jerusalem, and into the temple: and when he had looked round about upon all things, and now the eventide was come, he went out unto Bethany with the twelve.
12 ¶ And on the morrow, when they were come from Bethany, he was hungry:
13 And seeing a fig tree afar off having leaves, he came, if haply he might find any thing thereon: and when he came to it, he found nothing but leaves; for the time of figs was not *yet*.
14 And Jesus answered and said unto it, No man eat fruit of thee hereafter for ever. And his disciples heard *it*.

51 came to Jesus. And Jesus answered him, and said, What wilt thou that I should do unto thee? And the blind man said unto him, ¹Rabboni, that I may 52 receive my sight. And Jesus said unto him, Go thy way; thy faith hath ²made thee whole. And straightway he received his sight, and followed him in the way.

¹ See John xx. 16.
² Or, saved thee

11 And when they draw nigh unto Jerusalem, unto Bethphage and Bethany, at the mount of Olives, he 2 sendeth two of his disciples, and saith unto them, Go your way into the village that is over against you: and straightway as ye enter into it, ye shall find a colt tied, whereon no man ever yet sat; loose him, and bring 3 him. And if any one say unto you, Why do ye this? say ye, The Lord hath need of him; and straightway 4 he ³will send him ⁴back hither. And they went away, and found a colt tied at the door without in the open 5 street; and they loose him. And certain of them that stood there said unto them, What do ye, loosing the 6 colt? And they said unto them even as Jesus had 7 said: and they let them go. And they bring the colt unto Jesus, and cast on him their garments; and he 8 sat upon him. And many spread their garments upon the way; and others ⁵branches, which they had cut 9 from the fields. And they that went before, and they that followed, cried, Hosanna; Blessed is he that 10 cometh in the name of the Lord: Blessed is the kingdom that cometh, *the kingdom* of our father David: Hosanna in the highest.

³ Gr. *sendeth.*
⁴ Or, *again*

⁵ Gr. *layers of leaves.*

11 And he entered into Jerusalem, into the temple; and when he had looked round about upon all things, it being now eventide, he went out unto Bethany with the twelve.

12 And on the morrow, when they were come out from 13 Bethany, he hungered. And seeing a fig tree afar off having leaves, he came, if haply he might find anything thereon: and when he came to it, he found nothing but leaves; for it was not the season of figs. 14 And he answered and said unto it, No man eat fruit from thee henceforward for ever. And his disciples heard it.

Eng. Revision	K. James Vers.

Eng. Revision

15 And they come to Jerusalem: and he entered into the temple, and began to cast out them that sold and them that bought in the temple, and overthrew the tables of the money-changers, and the seats of them that sold the doves;
16 and he would not suffer that any man should carry a vessel through the temple.
17 And he taught, and said unto them, Is it not written, My house shall be called a house of prayer for all the nations? but ye have made it a den of
18 robbers. And the chief priests and the scribes heard it, and sought how they might destroy him: for they feared him, for all the multitude was astonished at his teaching.
19 And ¹ every evening ² he went forth out of the city.
20 And as they passed by in the morning, they saw the fig tree withered
21 away from the roots. And Peter calling to remembrance saith unto him, Rabbi, behold, the fig tree which thou
22 cursedst is withered away. And Jesus answering saith unto them, Have faith
23 in God. Verily I say unto you, Whosoever shall say unto this mountain, Be thou taken up and cast into the sea; and shall not doubt in his heart, but shall believe that what he saith cometh
24 to pass: he shall have it. Therefore I say unto you, All things whatsoever ye pray and ask for, believe that ye have received them, and ye shall have them.
25 And whensoever ye stand praying, forgive, if ye have aught against any one; that your Father also which is in heaven may forgive you your trespasses. ³
27 And they come again to Jerusalem: and as he was walking in the temple, there come to him the chief priests, and
28 the scribes, and the elders; and they said unto him, By what authority doest thou these things? or who gave thee this
29 authority to do these things? And Jesus said unto them, I will ask of you one ⁴ question, and answer me, and I will tell you by what authority I do
30 these things. The baptism of John, was it from heaven, or from men? an-
31 swer me. And they reasoned with themselves, saying, If we shall say, From heaven; he will say, Why then
32 did ye not believe him? ⁵ But should we say, From men—they feared the

1 Gr. *whenever evening came.*
2 Some ancient authorities read *they.*
3 Many ancient authorities add ver. 26 *But if ye do not forgive, neither will your Father which is in heaven forgive your trespasses.*
4 Gr. *word.*
5 Or, *But shall we say, From men?*

K. James Vers.

15 ¶ And they come to Jerusalem: and Jesus went into the temple, and began to cast out them that sold and bought in the temple, and overthrew the tables of the money changers, and the seats of them that sold doves;
16 And would not suffer that any man should carry *any* vessel through the temple.
17 And he taught, saying unto them, Is it not written, My house shall be called of all nations the house of prayer? but ye have made it a den of thieves.
18 And the scribes and chief priests heard *it*, and sought how they might destroy him: for they feared him, because all the people was astonished at his doctrine.
19 And when even was come, he went out of the city.
20 ¶ And in the morning, as they passed by, they saw the fig tree dried up from the roots.
21 And Peter calling to remembrance saith unto him, Master, behold, the fig tree which thou cursedst is withered away.
22 And Jesus answering saith unto them, Have faith in God.
23 For verily I say unto you, That whosoever shall say unto this mountain, Be thou removed, and be thou cast into the sea; and shall not doubt in his heart, but shall believe that those things which he saith shall come to pass; he shall have whatsoever he saith.
24 Therefore I say unto you, What things soever ye desire, when ye pray, believe that ye receive *them*, and ye shall have *them*.
25 And when ye stand praying, forgive, if ye have aught against any: that your Father also which is in heaven may forgive you your trespasses.
26 But if ye do not forgive, neither will your Father which is in heaven forgive your trespasses.
27 ¶ And they come again to Jerusalem: and as he was walking in the temple, there come to him the chief priests, and the scribes, and the elders,
28 And say unto him, By what authority doest thou these things? and who gave thee this authority to do these things?
29 And Jesus answered and said unto them, I will also ask of you one question, and answer me, and I will tell you by what authority I do these things.
30 The baptism of John, was *it* from heaven, or of men? answer me.
31 And they reasoned with themselves, saying, If we shall say, From heaven; he will say, Why then did ye not believe him?
32 But if we shall say, Of men; they

15 And they come to Jerusalem: and he entered into the temple, and began to cast out them that sold and them that bought in the temple, and overthrew the tables of the money-changers, and the seats of them
16 that sold the doves; and he would not suffer that any
17 man should carry a vessel through the temple. And he taught, and said unto them, Is it not written, My house shall be called a house of prayer for all the
18 nations? but ye have made it a den of robbers. And the chief priests and the scribes heard it, and sought how they might destroy him: for they feared him, for all the multitude was astonished at his teaching.
19 And ¹every evening ²he went forth out of the city.
20 And as they passed by in the morning, they saw the
21 fig tree withered away from the roots. And Peter calling to remembrance saith unto him, Rabbi, behold,
22 the fig tree which thou cursedst is withered away. And Jesus answering saith unto them, Have faith in God.
23 Verily I say unto you, Whosoever shall say unto this mountain, Be thou taken up and cast into the sea; and shall not doubt in his heart, but shall believe that what he saith cometh to pass; he shall have it.
24 Therefore I say unto you, All things whatsoever ye pray and ask for, believe that ye ³receive them,
25 and ye shall have them. And whensoever ye stand praying, forgive, if ye have aught against any one; that your Father also who is in heaven may forgive you your trespasses.⁴
27 And they come again to Jerusalem: and as he was walking in the temple, there come to him the chief
28 priests, and the scribes, and the elders; and they said unto him, By what authority doest thou these things? or who gave thee this authority to do these things?
29 And Jesus said unto them, I will ask of you one ⁵question, and answer me, and I will tell you by what
30 authority I do these things. The baptism of John,
31 was it from heaven, or from men? answer me. And they reasoned with themselves, saying, If we shall say, From heaven; he will say, Why then did ye not
32 believe him? ⁶But should we say, From men—they

¹ Gr. *when-ever evening came.*
² Some ancient authorities read *they.*
³ Gr. *received.*
⁴ Many ancient authorities add ver. 26 *But if ye do not forgive, neither will your Father who is in heaven forgive your trespasses.*
⁵ Gr. *word.*
⁶ Or, *But shall we say, From men?*

Eng. Revision.

people: [1] for all verily held John to be
33 a prophet. And they answered Jesus
and say, We know not. And Jesus
saith unto them, Neither tell I you by
what authority I do these things.
12 And he began to speak unto them in
parables. A man planted a vineyard,
and set a hedge about it, and digged a
pit for the winepress, and built a tower,
and let it out to husbandmen, and went
2 into another country. And at the season he sent to the husbandmen a [2] servant, that he might receive from the
husbandmen of the fruits of the vine-
3 yard. And they took him, and beat
4 him, and sent him away empty. And
again he sent unto them another [2] servant; and him they wounded in the
5 head, and handled shamefully. And
he sent another; and him they killed:
and many others; beating some, and
6 killing some. He had yet one, a beloved son: he sent him last unto them,
saying, They will reverence my son.
7 But those husbandmen said among
themselves, This is the heir; come, let
us kill him, and the inheritance shall
8 be ours. And they took him, and killed
him, and cast him forth out of the vine-
9 yard. What therefore will the lord of
the vineyard do? he will come and destroy the husbandmen, and will give
10 the vineyard unto others. Have ye
not read even this scripture;
The stone which the builders rejected,
The same was made the head of the corner:
11   This was from the Lord,
And it is marvellous in our eyes?
12 And they sought to lay hold on him;
and they feared the multitude; for they
perceived that he spake the parable
against them: and they left him, and
went away.
13   And they send unto him certain of
the Pharisees and of the Herodians,
14 that they might catch him in talk. And
when they were come, they say unto
him, [3] Master, we know that thou art
true, and carest not for any one: for
thou regardest not the person of men,
but of a truth teachest the way of God:
Is it lawful to give tribute unto Cæsar,
15 or not? Shall we give, or shall we not
give? But he, knowing their hypoc-

[1] Or, *for all held John to be a prophet indeed.*
[2] Gr. *bondservant.*
[3] Or, *Teacher*

S. MARK.

K. James Vers. 11. 32—

feared the people: for all *men* counted
John, that he was a prophet indeed.
33 And they answered and said unto
Jesus, We cannot tell. And Jesus answering saith unto them, Neither do I tell you
by what authority I do these things.

CHAPTER XII.

AND he began to speak unto them by
parables. A *certain* man planted a
vineyard, and set a hedge about *it*, and
digged *a place for* the winefat, and built a
tower, and let it out to husbandmen, and
went into a far country.
2 And at the season he sent to the
husbandmen a servant, that he might
receive from the husbandmen of the fruit
of the vineyard.
3 And they caught *him*, and beat him,
and sent *him* away empty.
4 And again he sent unto them another
servant; and at him they cast stones, and
wounded *him* in the head, and sent *him*
away shamefully handled.
5 And again he sent another; and him
they killed, and many others; beating
some, and killing some.
6 Having yet therefore one son, his well
beloved, he sent him also last unto them,
saying, They will reverence my son.
7 But those husbandmen said among
themselves, This is the heir; come, let us
kill him, and the inheritance shall be
ours.
8 And they took him, and killed *him*,
and cast *him* out of the vineyard.
9 What shall therefore the lord of the
vineyard do? he will come and destroy the
husbandmen, and will give the vineyard
unto others.
10 And have ye not read this Scripture;
The stone which the builders rejected is
become the head of the corner:
11 This was the Lord's doing, and it is
marvellous in our eyes?
12 And they sought to lay hold on him,
but feared the people; for they knew that
he had spoken the parable against them:
and they left him, and went their way.
13 ¶ And they send unto him certain of
the Pharisees and of the Herodians, to
catch him in *his* words.
14 And when they were come, they say
unto him, Master, we know that thou art
true, and carest for no man; for thou regardest not the person of men, but teachest
the way of God in truth: Is it lawful to
give tribute to Cesar, or not?
15 Shall we give, or shall we not give?
But he, knowing their hypocrisy, said

feared the people: ¹for all verily held John to be a ¹ Or, *for all held John to be a prophet indeed.*
33 prophet. And they answered Jesus and say, We know
not. And Jesus saith unto them, Neither tell I you
by what authority I do these things.
12 And he began to speak unto them in parables. A
man planted a vineyard, and set a hedge about it, and
digged a pit for the winepress, and built a tower, and
let it out to husbandmen, and went into another
2 country. And at the season he sent to the husband-
men a ²servant, that he might receive from the husband- ² Gr. *bondservant.*
3 men of the fruits of the vineyard. And they took him,
4 and beat him, and sent him away empty. And again
he sent unto them another ²servant; and him they
5 wounded in the head, and handled shamefully. And
he sent another; and him they killed: and many
6 others; beating some, and killing some. He had yet
one, a beloved son: he sent him last unto them,
7 saying, They will reverence my son. But those
husbandmen said among themselves, This is the heir;
come, let us kill him, and the inheritance shall be
8 ours. And they took him, and killed him, and cast
9 him forth out of the vineyard. What therefore will
the lord of the vineyard do? he will come and destroy
the husbandmen, and will give the vineyard unto
10 others. Have ye not read even this scripture;
The stone which the builders rejected,
The same was made the head of the corner:
11 This was from the Lord,
And it is marvellous in our eyes?
12 And they sought to lay hold on him; and they
feared the multitude; for they perceived that he spake
the parable against them: and they left him, and went
away.
13 And they send unto him certain of the Pharisees
and of the Herodians, that they might catch him in
14 talk. And when they were come, they say unto him,
³Master, we know that thou art true, and carest not ³ Or, *Teacher*
for any one: for thou regardest not the person of men,
but of a truth teachest the way of God: Is it lawful
to give tribute unto Cæsar, or not? Shall we give, or
15 shall we not give? But he, knowing their hypocrisy,

Eng. Revision.

risy, said unto them, Why tempt ye me? bring me a ¹penny, that I may
16 see it. And they brought it. And he saith unto them, Whose is this image and superscription? And they said
17 unto him, Cæsar's. And Jesus said unto them, Render unto Cæsar the things that are Cæsar's, and unto God the things that are God's. And they marvelled greatly at him.
18 And there come unto him Sadducees, which say that there is no resurrection;
19 and they asked him, saying, ²Master, Moses wrote unto us, If a man's brother die, and leave a wife behind him, and leave no child, that his brother should take his wife, and raise up seed
20 unto his brother. There were seven brethren: and the first took a wife, and
21 dying left no seed; and the second took her, and died, leaving no seed be-
22 hind him; and the third likewise: and the seven left no seed. Last of all the
23 woman also died. In the resurrection whose wife shall she be of them? for
24 the seven had her to wife. Jesus said unto them, Is it not for this cause that ye err, that ye know not the scriptures,
25 nor the power of God? For when they shall rise from the dead, they neither marry, nor are given in marriage; but
26 are as angels in heaven. But as touching the dead, that they are raised; have ye not read in the book of Moses, in *the place concerning* the Bush, how God spake unto him, saying, I *am* the God of Abraham, and the God of Isaac,
27 and the God of Jacob? He is not the God of the dead, but of the living: ye do greatly err.
28 And one of the scribes came, and heard them questioning together, and knowing that he had answered them well, asked him, What commandment
29 is the first of all? Jesus answered, The first is, Hear, O Israel; ³The Lord our
30 God, the Lord is one: and thou shalt love the Lord thy God ⁴with all thy heart, and ⁴with all thy soul, and ⁴with all thy mind, and ⁴with all thy
31 strength. The second is this, Thou shalt love thy neighbour as thyself. There is none other commandment
32 greater than these. And the scribe said unto him, Of a truth, ²Master, thou hast well said that he is one; and

1 See marginal note on Matt. xviii. 28.
2 Or, *Teacher*
3 Or, *The Lord is our God ; the Lord is one*
4 Gr. *from.*

K. James Vers.

unto them, Why tempt ye me? bring me a penny, that I may see *it*.
16 And they brought *it*. And he saith unto them, Whose *is* this image and superscription? And they said unto him, Cesar's.
17 And Jesus answering said unto them, Render to Cesar the things that are Cesar's, and to God the things that are God's. And they marvelled at him.
18 ¶ Then come unto him the Sadducees, which say there is no resurrection; and they asked him, saying,
19 Master, Moses wrote unto us, If a man's brother die, and leave *his* wife *behind him*, and leave no children, that his brother should take his wife, and raise up seed unto his brother.
20 Now there were seven brethren: and the first took a wife, and dying left no seed.
21 And the second took her, and died, neither left he any seed: and the third likewise.
22 And the seven had her, and left no seed: last of all the woman died also.
23 In the resurrection therefore, when they shall rise, whose wife shall she be of them? for the seven had her to wife.
24 And Jesus answering said unto them, Do ye not therefore err, because ye know not the Scriptures, neither the power of God?
25 For when they shall rise from the dead, they neither marry, nor are given in marriage; but are as the angels which are in heaven.
26 And as touching the dead, that they rise; have ye not read in the book of Moses, how in the bush God spake unto him, saying, I *am* the God of Abraham, and the God of Isaac, and the God of Jacob?
27 He is not the God of the dead, but the God of the living: ye therefore do greatly err.
28 ¶ And one of the scribes came, and having heard them reasoning together, and perceiving that he had answered them well, asked him, Which is the first commandment of all?
29 And Jesus answered him, The first of all the commandments *is*, Hear, O Israel; The Lord our God is one Lord:
30 And thou shalt love the Lord thy God with all thy heart, and with all thy soul, and with all thy mind, and with all thy strength: this *is* the first commandment.
31 And the second *is* like, *namely* this, Thou shalt love thy neighbour as thyself. There is none other commandment greater than these.
32 And the scribe said unto him, Well, Master, thou hast said the truth: for there

said unto them, Why try ye me? bring me a
16 ¹denarius, that I may see it. And they brought it. ¹See marginal note on Matt. xviii. 28.
And he saith unto them, Whose is this image and
superscription? And they said unto him, Cæsar's.
17 And Jesus said unto them, Render unto Cæsar the
things that are Cæsar's, and unto God the things that
are God's. And they marvelled greatly at him.
18 And there come unto him Sadducees, who say
that there is no resurrection; and they asked him,
19 saying, ²Master, Moses wrote unto us, If a man's ²Or, Teacher
brother die, and leave a wife behind him, and leave
no child, that his brother should take his wife, and
20 raise up seed unto his brother. There were seven
brethren: and the first took a wife, and dying left no
21 seed; and the second took her, and died, leaving no
22 seed behind him; and the third likewise: and the
seven left no seed. Last of all the woman also died.
23 In the resurrection whose wife shall she be of them?
24 for the seven had her to wife. Jesus said unto them,
Is it not for this cause that ye err, that ye know not
25 the scriptures, nor the power of God? For when
they shall rise from the dead, they neither marry, nor
are given in marriage; but are as angels in heaven.
26 But as touching the dead, that they are raised; have ye
not read in the book of Moses, in *the place concerning
the Bush*, how God spake unto him, saying, I am the
God of Abraham, and the God of Isaac, and the God
27 of Jacob? He is not the God of the dead, but of the
living: ye do greatly err.
28 And one of the scribes came, and heard them
questioning together, and knowing that he had
answered them well, asked him, What command-
29 ment is the first of all? Jesus answered, The first
is, Hear, O Israel; ³The Lord our God, the Lord is ³Or, *The Lord is our God; the Lord is one*
30 one: and thou shalt love the Lord thy God ⁴with all
thy heart, and ⁴with all thy soul, and ⁴with all thy ⁴Gr. *from*.
31 mind, and ⁴with all thy strength. The second is this,
Thou shalt love thy neighbour as thyself. There is
32 none other commandment greater than these. And
the scribe said unto him, Of a truth, ²Master, thou hast
well said that he is one; and there is none other but

Eng. Revision.

33 there is none other but he: and to love him with all the heart, and with all the understanding, and with all the strength, and to love his neighbour as himself, is much more than all whole
34 burnt offerings and sacrifices. And when Jesus saw that he answered discreetly, he said unto him, Thou art not far from the kingdom of God. And no man after that durst ask him any question.
35 And Jesus answered and said, as he taught in the temple, How say the scribes that the Christ is the son of
36 David? David himself said in the Holy Spirit,
The Lord said unto my Lord,
Sit thou on my right hand,
Till I make thine enemies [1] the footstool of thy feet.
37 David himself calleth him Lord; and whence is he his son? And [2] the common people heard him gladly.
38 And in his teaching he said, Beware of the scribes, which desire to walk in long robes, and *to have* salutations in
39 the marketplaces, and chief seats in the synagogues, and chief places at
40 feasts: they which devour widows' houses, [3] and for a pretence make long prayers; these shall receive greater condemnation.
41 And he sat down over against the treasury, and beheld how the multitude cast [4] money into the treasury: and many that were rich cast in much.
42 And there came [5] a poor widow, and she cast in two mites, which make a
43 farthing. And he called unto him his disciples, and said unto them, Verily I say unto you, This poor widow cast in more than all they which are casting
44 into the treasury: for they all did cast in of their superfluity; but she of her want did cast in all that she had, *even* all her living.
13 And as he went forth out of the temple, one of his disciples saith unto him, [6] Master, behold, what manner of stones and what manner of buildings!
2 And Jesus said unto him, Seest thou these great buildings? there shall not be left here one stone upon another, which shall not be thrown down.
3 And as he sat on the mount of Olives over against the temple, Peter and James and John and Andrew asked

---
[1] Some ancient authorities read *underneath thy feet.*
[2] Or, *the great multitude*
[3] Or, *even while for a pretence they make*
[4] Gr. *brass.*
[5] Gr. *one.*
[6] Or, *Teacher*

K. James Vers. 12. 32—

is one God; and there is none other but he:
33 And to love him with all the heart, and with all the understanding, and with all the soul, and with all the strength, and to love *his* neighbour as himself, is more than all whole burnt offerings and sacrifices.
34 And when Jesus saw that he answered discreetly, he said unto him, Thou art not far from the kingdom of God. And no man after that durst ask him *any question.*
35 ¶ And Jesus answered and said, while he taught in the temple, How say the scribes that Christ is the son of David?
36 For David himself said by the Holy Ghost, The LORD said to my Lord, Sit thou on my right hand, till I make thine enemies thy footstool.
37 David therefore himself calleth him Lord; and whence is he *then* his son? And the common people heard him gladly.
38 ¶ And he said unto them in his doctrine, Beware of the scribes, which love to go in long clothing, and *love* salutations in the marketplaces,
39 And the chief seats in the synagogues, and the uppermost rooms at feasts:
40 Which devour widows' houses, and for a pretence make long prayers: these shall receive greater damnation.
41 ¶ And Jesus sat over against the treasury, and beheld how the people cast money into the treasury: and many that were rich cast in much.
42 And there came a certain poor widow, and she threw in two mites, which make a farthing.
43 And he called *unto him* his disciples, and saith unto them, Verily I say unto you, That this poor widow hath cast more in, than all they which have cast into the treasury:
44 For all *they* did cast in of their abundance; but she of her want did cast in all that she had, *even* all her living.

CHAPTER XIII.

AND as he went out of the temple, one of his disciples saith unto him, Master, see what manner of stones and what buildings *are here!*
2 And Jesus answering said unto him, Seest thou these great buildings? there shall not be left one stone upon another, that shall not be thrown down.
3 And as he sat upon the mount of Olives, over against the temple, Peter and James and John and Andrew asked him privately,

33 he : and to love him with all the heart, and with all the understanding, and with all the strength, and to love his neighbour as himself, is much more than all
34 whole burnt offerings and sacrifices. And when Jesus saw that he answered discreetly, he said unto him, Thou art not far from the kingdom of God. And no man after that durst ask him any question.
35 And Jesus answered and said, as he taught in the temple, How say the scribes that the Christ is the son
36 of David? David himself said in the Holy Spirit,
The Lord said unto my Lord,
Sit thou on my right hand,
Till I make thine enemies [1] the footstool of thy feet.
37 David himself calleth him Lord; and whence is he his son? And [2] the common people heard him gladly.
38 And in his teaching he said, Beware of the scribes, who desire to walk in long robes, and *to have* salu-
39 tations in the marketplaces, and chief seats in the
40 synagogues, and chief places at feasts: they who devour widows' houses, [3] and for a pretence make long prayers; these shall receive greater condemnation.
41 And he sat down over against the treasury, and beheld how the multitude cast [4] money into the treasury: and many that were rich cast in much.
42 And there came [5] a poor widow, and she cast in two
43 mites, which make a farthing. And he called unto him his disciples, and said unto them, Verily I say unto you, This poor widow cast in more than all they
44 that are casting into the treasury: for they all did cast in of their superfluity: but she of her want did cast in all that she had, *even* all her living.

13 And as he went forth out of the temple, one of his disciples saith unto him, [6] Master, behold, what manner
2 of stones and what manner of buildings! And Jesus said unto him, Seest thou these great buildings? there shall not be left here one stone upon another, which shall not be thrown down.
3 And as he sat on the mount of Olives over against the temple, Peter and James and John and Andrew

[1] Some ancient authorities read *underneath thy feet*.
[2] Or, *the great multitude*
[3] Or, *even while for a pretence*
[4] Gr. *brass*.
[5] Gr. *one*.
[6] Or, *Teacher*

Eng. Revision.

4 him privately, Tell us, when shall these things be? and what *shall be* the sign when these things are all about to be 5 accomplished? And Jesus began to say unto them, Take heed that no man lead 6 you astray. Many shall come in my name, saying, I am *he*; and shall lead 7 many astray. And when ye shall hear of wars and rumours of wars, be not troubled: *these things* must needs come 8 to pass; but the end is not yet. For nation shall rise against nation, and kingdom against kingdom: there shall be earthquakes in divers places; there shall be famines: these things are the beginning of travail.
9 But take ye heed to yourselves: for they shall deliver you up to councils; and in synagogues shall ye be beaten; and before governors and kings shall ye stand for my sake, for a testimony 10 unto them. And the gospel must first 11 be preached unto all the nations. And when they lead you *to judgement,* and deliver you up, be not anxious beforehand what ye shall speak: but whatsoever shall be given you in that hour, that speak ye: for it is not ye that 12 speak, but the Holy Ghost. And brother shall deliver up brother to death, and the father his child; and children shall rise up against parents, and 13 [1] cause them to be put to death. And ye shall be hated of all men for my name's sake: but he that endureth to the end, the same shall be saved.
14 But when ye see the abomination of desolation standing where he ought not (let him that readeth understand), then let them that are in Judæa flee 15 unto the mountains: and let him that is on the housetop not go down, nor enter in, to take anything out of his 16 house: and let him that is in the field 17 not return back to take his cloke. But woe unto them that are with child and to them that give suck in those days!
18 And pray ye that it be not in the winter.
19 For those days shall be tribulation, such as there hath not been the like from the beginning of the creation which God created until now, and 20 never shall be. And except the Lord had shortened the days, no flesh would have been saved: but for the elect's

---
[1] Or, *put them to death*

S. MARK. K. James Vers. 13. 3—

4 Tell us, when shall these things be? and what *shall be* the sign when all these things shall be fulfilled?
5 And Jesus answering them began to say, Take heed lest any *man* deceive you: 6 For many shall come in my name saying, I am *Christ;* and shall deceive many.
7 And when ye shall hear of wars and rumours of wars, be ye not troubled: for *such things* must needs be; but the end shall not be yet.
8 For nation shall rise against nation, and kingdom against kingdom: and there shall be earthquakes in divers places, and there shall be famines and troubles: these *are* the beginnings of sorrows.
9 ¶ But take heed to yourselves: for they shall deliver you up to councils; and in the synagogues ye shall be beaten: and ye shall be brought before rulers and kings for my sake, for a testimony against them.
10 And the gospel must first be published among all nations.
11 But when they shall lead *you,* and deliver you up, take no thought beforehand what ye shall speak, neither do ye premeditate: but whatsoever shall be given you in that hour, that speak ye: for it is not ye that speak, but the Holy Ghost.
12 Now the brother shall betray the brother to death, and the father the son; and children shall rise up against *their* parents, and shall cause them to be put to death.
13 And ye shall be hated of all *men* for my name's sake: but he that shall endure unto the end, the same shall be saved.
14 ¶ But when ye shall see the abomination of desolation, spoken of by Daniel the prophet, standing where it ought not, (let him that readeth understand,) then let them that be in Judea flee to the mountains:
15 And let him that is on the housetop not go down into the house, neither enter *therein,* to take any thing out of his house:
16 And let him that is in the field not turn back again for to take up his garment.
17 But woe to them that are with child, and to them that give suck in those days!
18 And pray ye that your flight be not in the winter.
19 For *in* those days shall be affliction, such as was not from the beginning of the creation which God created unto this time, neither shall be.
20 And except that the Lord had shortened those days, no flesh should be saved:

4 asked him privately, Tell us, when shall these things be? and what *shall be* the sign when these things are
5 all about to be accomplished? And Jesus began to say unto them, Take heed that no man lead you
6 astray. Many shall come in my name, saying, I am
7 *he*; and shall lead many astray. And when ye shall hear of wars and rumours of wars, be not troubled: *these things* must needs come to pass; but the end is
8 not yet. For nation shall rise against nation, and kingdom against kingdom: there shall be earthquakes in divers places; there shall be famines: these things are the beginning of travail.
9 But take ye heed to yourselves: for they shall deliver you up to councils; and in synagogues shall ye be beaten; and before governors and kings shall ye stand for my sake, for a testimony unto them.
10 And the gospel must first be preached unto all the
11 nations. And when they lead you *to judgement*, and deliver you up, be not anxious beforehand what ye shall speak: but whatsoever shall be given you in that hour, that speak ye: for it is not ye that speak,
12 but the Holy Spirit. And brother shall deliver up brother to death, and the father his child; and children shall rise up against parents, and [1] cause
13 them to be put to death. And ye shall be hated of all men for my name's sake: but he that endureth to the end, the same shall be saved.
14 But when ye see the abomination of desolation standing where he ought not (let him that readeth understand), then let them that are in Judæa flee
15 unto the mountains: and let him that is on the housetop not go down, nor enter in, to take any-
16 thing out of his house: and let him that is in the field
17 not return back to take his cloke. But woe unto them that are with child and to them that give suck in
18 those days! And pray ye that it be not in the winter.
19 For those days shall be tribulation, such as there hath not been the like from the beginning of the creation which God created until now, and never shall be.
20 And except the Lord had shortened the days, no flesh would have been saved: but for the elect's sake,

[1] Or, *put them to death*

Eng. Revision.

sake, whom he chose, he shortened the
21 days. And then if any man shall say
unto you, Lo, here is the Christ; or,
22 Lo, there; believe ¹*it* not: for there
shall arise false Christs and false prophets, and shall shew signs and wonders,
that they may lead astray, if pos-
23 sible, the elect. But take ye heed:
behold, I have told you all things beforehand.
24 But in those days, after that tribulation, the sun shall be darkened, and
25 the moon shall not give her light, and
the stars shall be falling from heaven,
and the powers that are in the heavens
26 shall be shaken. And then shall they
see the Son of man coming in clouds
27 with great power and glory. And then
shall he send forth the angels, and
shall gather together his elect from
the four winds, from the uttermost
part of the earth to the uttermost part
of heaven.
28 Now from the fig tree learn her parable: when her branch is now become
tender, and putteth forth its leaves, ye
29 know that the summer is nigh; even so
ye also, when ye see these things coming to pass, know ye that ²he is nigh,
30 *even* at the doors. Verily I say unto
you, This generation shall not pass
away, until all these things be accom-
31 plished. Heaven and earth shall pass
away: but my words shall not pass
32 away. But of that day or that hour
knoweth no one, not even the angels in
heaven, neither the Son, but the Fa-
33 ther. Take ye heed, watch ³ and pray:
34 for ye know not when the time is. *It is*
as *when* a man, sojourning in another
country, having left his house, and
given authority to his ⁴ servants, to
each one his work, commanded also
35 the porter to watch. Watch therefore:
for ye know not when the lord of the
house cometh, whether at even, or at
midnight, or at cockcrowing, or in the
36 morning; lest coming suddenly he find
37 you sleeping. And what I say unto
you I say unto all, Watch.
14 Now after two days was *the feast of*
the passover and the unleavened
bread: and the chief priests and the
scribes sought how they might take
2 him with subtilty, and kill him: for
they said, Not during the feast, lest
haply there shall be a tumult of the
people.

1 Or, him
2 Or, *it*
3 Some ancient authorities omit *and pray*.
4 Gr. *bondservants*.

S. MARK.   K. James Vers. 13. 20—

but for the elect's sake, whom he hath
chosen, he hath shortened the days.
21 And then if any man shall say to you,
Lo, here *is* Christ; or, lo, *he is* there; believe *him* not:
22 For false Christs and false prophets
shall rise, and shall shew signs and wonders, to seduce, if *it were* possible, even
the elect.
23 But take ye heed: behold, I have
foretold you all things.
24 ¶ But in those days, after that tribulation, the sun shall be darkened, and the
moon shall not give her light,
25 And the stars of heaven shall fall, and
the powers that are in heaven shall be
shaken.
26 And then shall they see the Son of
man coming in the clouds with great
power and glory.
27 And then shall he send his angels,
and shall gather together his elect from
the four winds, from the uttermost part of
the earth to the uttermost part of heaven.
28 Now learn a parable of the fig tree:
When her branch is yet tender, and putteth forth leaves, ye know that summer is
near:
29 So ye in like manner, when ye shall
see these things come to pass, know that
it is nigh, *even* at the doors.
30 Verily I say unto you, that this generation shall not pass, till all these things
be done.
31 Heaven and earth shall pass away:
but my words shall not pass away.
32 ¶ But of that day and *that* hour
knoweth no man, no, not the angels which
are in heaven, neither the Son, but the
Father.
33 Take ye heed, watch and pray: for
ye know not when the time is.
34 *For the Son of man is* as a man taking a far journey, who left his house, and
gave authority to his servants, and to
every man his work, and commanded the
porter to watch.
35 Watch ye therefore: for ye know not
when the master of the house cometh, at
even, or at midnight, or at the cockcrowing, or in the morning:
36 Lest coming suddenly he find you
sleeping.
37 And what I say unto you I say unto
all, Watch.

CHAPTER XIV.

AFTER two days was *the feast of* the
passover, and of unleavened bread:
and the chief priests and the scribes
sought how they might take him by craft,
and put *him* to death.
2 But they said, Not on the feast *day*,
lest there be an uproar of the people.

21 whom he chose, he shortened the days. And then if any man shall say unto you, Lo, here is the Christ; or,
22 Lo, there; believe ¹*it* not: for there shall arise false Christs and false prophets, and shall shew signs and wonders, that they may lead astray, if possible, the
23 elect. But take ye heed: behold, I have told you all things beforehand.
24 But in those days, after that tribulation, the sun shall be darkened, and the moon shall not give her
25 light, and the stars shall be falling from heaven, and the powers that are in the heavens shall be shaken.
26 And then shall they see the Son of man coming in
27 clouds with great power and glory. And then shall he send forth the angels, and shall gather together his elect from the four winds, from the uttermost part of the earth to the uttermost part of heaven.
28 Now from the fig tree learn her parable: when her branch is now become tender, and putteth forth its
29 leaves, ye know that the summer is nigh; even so ye also, when ye see these things coming to pass, know
30 ye that ²he is nigh, *even* at the doors. Verily I say unto you, This generation shall not pass away, until
31 all these things be accomplished. Heaven and earth shall pass away: but my words shall not pass away.
32 But of that day or that hour knoweth no one, not even the angels in heaven, neither the Son, but the
33 Father. Take ye heed, watch ³and pray: for ye
34 know not when the time is. *It is* as *when* a man, sojourning in another country, having left his house, and given authority to his ⁴servants, to each one his
35 work, commanded also the porter to watch. Watch therefore: for ye know not when the lord of the house cometh, whether at even, or at midnight, or at
36 cockcrowing, or in the morning; lest coming sud-
37 denly he find you sleeping. And what I say unto you I say unto all, Watch.

14 Now after two days was *the feast of* the passover and the unleavened bread: and the chief priests and the scribes sought how they might take him with sub-
2 tilty, and kill him: for they said, Not during the feast, lest haply there shall be a tumult of the people.

¹ Or, him

² Or, *it*

³ Some ancient authorities omit *and pray*.
⁴ Gr. *bondservants*.

Eng. Revision

3 And while he was in Bethany in the house of Simon the leper, as he sat at meat, there came a woman having [1] an alabaster cruse of ointment of [2] spikenard very costly; *and* she brake the cruse, and poured it over his head. 4 But there were some that had indignation among themselves, *saying*, To what purpose hath this waste of the ointment been made? 5 For this ointment might have been sold for above three hundred [3] pence, and given to the poor. And they murmured against her. 6 But Jesus said, Let her alone; why trouble ye her? she hath wrought a good work on me. 7 For ye have the poor always with you, and whensoever ye will ye can do them good: but me ye have not always. 8 She hath done what she could: she hath anointed my body aforehand for the burying. 9 And verily I say unto you, Wheresoever the gospel shall be preached throughout the whole world, that also which this woman hath done shall be spoken of for a memorial of her. 10 And Judas Iscariot, [4] he that was one of the twelve, went away unto the chief priests, that he might deliver him unto them. 11 And they, when they heard it, were glad, and promised to give him money. And he sought how he might conveniently deliver him *unto them*. 12 And on the first day of unleavened bread, when they sacrificed the passover, his disciples say unto him, Where wilt thou that we go and make ready that thou mayest eat the passover? 13 And he sendeth two of his disciples, and saith unto them, Go into the city, and there shall meet you a man bearing a pitcher of water: follow him; 14 and wheresoever he shall enter in, say to the goodman of the house, The [5] Master saith, Where is my guestchamber, where I shall eat the passover with my disciples? 15 And he will himself shew you a large upper room furnished *and* ready: and there make ready for us. 16 And the disciples went forth, and came into the city, and found as he had said unto them: and they made ready the passover. 17 And when it was evening he cometh 18 with the twelve. And as they [6] sat and were eating, Jesus said, Verily I say

---

1 Or, *a flask*
2 Gr. *pistic nard*, pistic being perhaps a local name. Others take it to mean *genuine*; others, *liquid*.
3 See marginal note on Matt. xviii. 28.
4 Gr. *the one of the twelve.*
5 Or, *Teacher*
6 Gr. *reclined.*

K. James Vers.

3 ¶ And being in Bethany, in the house of Simon the leper, as he sat at meat, there came a woman having an alabaster box of ointment of spikenard very precious; and she brake the box, and poured *it* on his head, 4 And there were some that had indignation within themselves, and said, Why was this waste of the ointment made? 5 For it might have been sold for more than three hundred pence, and have been given to the poor. And they murmured against her. 6 And Jesus said, Let her alone; why trouble ye her? she hath wrought a good work on me. 7 For ye have the poor with you always, and whensoever ye will ye may do them good: but me ye have not always. 8 She hath done what she could: she is come aforehand to anoint my body to the burying. 9 Verily I say unto you, Wheresover this gospel shall be preached throughout the whole world, *this* also that she hath done shall be spoken of for a memorial of her. 10 ¶ And Judas Iscariot, one of the twelve, went unto the chief priests, to betray him unto them. 11 And when they heard *it*, they were glad, and promised to give him money. And he sought how he might conveniently betray him. 12 ¶ And the first day of unleavened bread, when they killed the passover, his disciples said unto him, Where wilt thou that we go and prepare that thou mayest eat the passover? 13 And he sendeth forth two of his disciples, and saith unto them, Go ye into the city, and there shall meet you a man bearing a pitcher of water: follow him. 14 And wheresoever he shall go in, say ye to the goodman of the house, The Master saith, Where is the guestchamber, where I shall eat the passover with my disciples? 15 And he will shew you a large upper room furnished *and* prepared: there make ready for us. 16 And his disciples went forth, came into the city, and found as he said unto them: and they made ready the passover. 17 And in the evening he cometh with the twelve. 18 And as they sat and did eat,

3 And while he was in Bethany in the house of Simon the leper, as he sat at meat, there came a woman having ¹an alabaster cruse of ointment of ²pure nard very costly; *and* she brake the cruse, and 4 poured it over his head. But there were some that had indignation among themselves, *saying*, To what purpose hath this waste of the ointment been made? 5 For this ointment might have been sold for above three hundred ³shillings, and given to the poor. And 6 they murmured against her. But Jesus said, Let her alone; why trouble ye her? she hath wrought 7 a good work on me. For ye have the poor always with you, and whensoever ye will ye can do them 8 good: but me ye have not always. She hath done what she could: she hath anointed my body afore-9 hand for the burying. And verily I say unto you, Wheresoever the gospel shall be preached throughout the whole world, that also which this woman hath done shall be spoken of for a memorial of her.

10   And Judas Iscariot, ⁴he that was one of the twelve, went away unto the chief priests, that he might 11 deliver him unto them. And they, when they heard it, were glad, and promised to give him money. And he sought how he might conveniently deliver him *unto them.*

12   And on the first day of unleavened bread, when they sacrificed the passover, his disciples say unto him, Where wilt thou that we go and make ready that 13 thou mayest eat the passover? And he sendeth two of his disciples, and saith unto them, Go into the city, and there shall meet you a man bearing a pitcher 14 of water: follow him; and wheresoever he shall enter in, say to the goodman of the house, The ⁵Master saith, Where is my guest-chamber, where I shall eat 15 the passover with my disciples? And he will himself shew you a large upper room furnished *and* ready: 16 and there make ready for us. And the disciples went forth, and came into the city, and found as he had said unto them: and they made ready the passover.

17   And when it was evening he cometh with the twelve. 18 And as they ⁶sat and were eating, Jesus said, Verily

¹ Or, *a flask*
² Or, *liquid nard*

³ See marginal note on Matt. xviii. 28.

⁴ Gr. *the one of the twelve.*

⁵ Or, *Teacher*

⁶ Gr. *reclined.*

Eng. Revision.

unto you, One of you shall betray me,
19 *even* he that eateth with me. They
began to be sorrowful, and to say unto
20 him one by one, Is it I? And he said
unto them, *It is* one of the twelve, he
21 that dippeth with me in the dish. For
the Son of man goeth, even as it is
written of him: but woe unto that man
through whom the Son of man is betrayed! good were it [1] for that man if
he had not been born.
22 And as they were eating, he took
[2] bread, and when he had blessed, he
brake it, and gave to them, and said,
23 Take ye: this is my body. And he
took a cup, and when he had given
thanks, he gave to them: and they all
24 drank of it. And he said unto them,
This is my blood of [3] the [4] covenant,
25 which is shed for many. Verily I say
unto you, I will no more drink of the
fruit of the vine, until that day when I
drink it new in the kingdom of God.
26 And when they had sung a hymn, they
went out unto the mount of Olives.
27 And Jesus saith unto them, All ye
shall be [5] offended: for it is written, I
will smite the shepherd, and the sheep
28 shall be scattered abroad. Howbeit,
after I am raised up, I will go before
29 you into Galilee. But Peter said unto
him, Although all shall be [5] offended,
30 yet will not I. And Jesus saith unto
him, Verily I say unto thee, that thou
to-day, *even* this night, before the cock
31 crow twice, shalt deny me thrice. But
he spake exceeding vehemently, If I
must die with thee, I will not deny
thee. And in like manner also said
they all.
32 And they come unto [6] a place which
was named Gethsemane: and he saith
unto his disciples, Sit ye here, while I
33 pray. And he taketh with him Peter
and James and John, and began to
be greatly amazed, and sore troubled.
34 And he saith unto them, My soul is exceeding sorrowful even unto death:
35 abide ye here, and watch. And he
went forward a little, and fell on the
ground, and prayed that, if it were
possible, the hour might pass away
36 from him. And he said, Abba, Father,
all things are possible unto thee; re-
move this cup from me: howbeit not

[1] Gr. *for him if that man.*
[2] Or, *a loaf*
[3] Or, *the testament*
[4] Some ancient authorities insert *new.*
[5] Gr. *caused to stumble.*
[6] Gr. *an enclosed piece of ground.*

K. James Vers.

said, Verily I say unto you, One of you
which eateth with me shall betray me.
19 And they began to be sorrowful, and
to say unto him one by one, *Is* it I? and
another *said*, *Is* it I?
20 And he answered and said unto them,
It is one of the twelve, that dippeth with
me in the dish.
21 The Son of man indeed goeth, as it is
written of him: but woe to that man by
whom the Son of man is betrayed! good
were it for that man if he had never been
born.
22 ¶ And as they did eat, Jesus took
bread, and blessed, and brake *it*, and gave
to them, and said, Take, eat; this is my
body.
23 And he took the cup, and when he
had given thanks, he gave *it* to them: and
they all drank of it.
24 And he said unto them, This is my
blood of the new testament, which is shed
for many.
25 Verily I say unto you, I will drink no
more of the fruit of the vine, until that
day that I drink it new in the kingdom of
God.
26 ¶ And when they had sung a hymn,
they went out into the mount of Olives.
27 And Jesus saith unto them, All ye
shall be offended because of me this night:
for it is written, I will smite the Shepherd,
and the sheep shall be scattered.
28 But after that I am risen, I will go
before you into Galilee.
29 But Peter said unto him, Although
all shall be offended, yet *will* not I.
30 And Jesus saith unto him, Verily I
say unto thee, That this day, *even* in this
night, before the cock crow twice, thou
shalt deny me thrice.
31 But he spake the more vehemently,
If I should die with thee, I will not deny
thee in any wise. Likewise also said they
all.
32 And they came to a place which was
named Gethsemane: and he saith to his
disciples, Sit ye here, while I shall pray.
33 And he taketh with him Peter and
James and John, and began to be sore
amazed, and to be very heavy;
34 And saith unto them, My soul is exceeding sorrowful unto death: tarry ye
here, and watch.
35 And he went forward a little, and fell
on the ground, and prayed that, if it were
possible, the hour might pass from him.
36 And he said, Abba, Father, all things
are possible unto thee; take away this
cup from me : nevertheless, not what I
will, but what thou wilt.

I say unto you, One of you shall betray me, *even* he
19 that eateth with me. They began to be sorrowful,
20 and to say unto him one by one, Is it I? And he said
unto them, *It is* one of the twelve, he that dippeth
21 with me in the dish. For the Son of man goeth, even
as it is written of him: but woe unto that man
through whom the Son of man is betrayed! good
were it [1] for that man if he had not been born.
22 And as they were eating, he took [2] bread, and when
he had blessed, he brake it, and gave to them, and
23 said, Take ye: this is my body. And he took a cup,
and when he had given thanks, he gave to them: and
24 they all drank of it. And he said unto them, This is
my blood of the [3] covenant, which is shed for many.
25 Verily I say unto you, I shall no more drink of the
fruit of the vine, until that day when I drink it new in
the kingdom of God.
26 And when they had sung a hymn, they went out
unto the mount of Olives.
27 And Jesus saith unto them, All ye shall be [4] offended:
for it is written, I will smite the shepherd, and the
28 sheep shall be scattered abroad. Howbeit, after I am
29 raised up, I will go before you into Galilee. But
Peter said unto him, Although all shall be [4] offended,
30 yet will not I. And Jesus saith unto him, Verily
I say unto thee, that thou to-day, *even* this night, be-
31 fore the cock crow twice, shalt deny me thrice. But he
spake exceeding vehemently, If I must die with thee,
I will not deny thee. And in like manner also said
they all.
32 And they come unto [5] a place which was named
Gethsemane: and he saith unto his disciples, Sit ye
33 here, while I pray. And he taketh with him Peter
and James and John, and began to be greatly amazed,
34 and sore troubled. And he saith unto them, My soul
is exceeding sorrowful even unto death: abide ye
35 here, and watch. And he went forward a little, and
fell on the ground, and prayed that, if it were possible,
36 the hour might pass away from him. And he said,
Abba, Father, all things are possible unto thee; re-
move this cup from me: howbeit not what I will, but

[1] Gr. *for him if that man.*
[2] Or, *a loaf*
[3] Some ancient authorities insert *new.*
[4] Gr. *caused to stumble.*
[5] Gr. *an enclosed piece of ground.*

Eng. Revision	K. James Vers.
37 what I will, but what thou wilt. And he cometh, and findeth them sleeping, and saith unto Peter, Simon, sleepest thou? couldest thou not watch one 38 hour? ¹ Watch and pray, that ye enter not into temptation: the spirit indeed 39 is willing, but the flesh is weak. And again he went away, and prayed, say-40 ing the same words. And again he came, and found them sleeping, for their eyes were very heavy; and they 41 wist not what to answer him. And he cometh the third time, and saith unto them, Sleep on now, and take your rest: it is enough; the hour is come; behold, the Son of man is betrayed into 42 the hands of sinners. Arise, let us be going: behold, he that betrayeth me is at hand. 43 And straightway, while he yet spake, cometh Judas, one of the twelve, and with him a multitude with swords and staves, from the chief priests and the 44 scribes and the elders. Now he that betrayed him had given them a token, saying, Whomsoever I shall kiss, that is he: take him, and lead him away safely. 45 And when he was come, straightway he came to him, and saith, Rabbi; and 46 ² kissed him. And they laid hands on 47 him, and took him. But a certain one of them that stood by drew his sword, and smote the ³ servant of the high 48 priest, and struck off his ear. And Jesus answered and said unto them, Are ye come out, as against a robber, 49 with swords and staves to seize me? I was daily with you in the temple teach-ing, and ye took me not: but *this is done* that the scriptures might be ful-50 filled. And they all left him, and fled. 51 And a certain young man followed with him, having a linen cloth cast about him, over *his* naked *body:* and 52 they lay hold on him; but he left the linen cloth, and fled naked. 53 And they led Jesus away to the high priest: and there come together with him all the chief priests and the elders 54 and the scribes. And Peter had fol-lowed him afar off, even within, into the court of the high priest; and he was sitting with the officers, and warming 55 himself in the light *of the fire.* Now the chief priests and the whole council sought witness against Jesus to put him 56 to death; and found it not. For many	37 And he cometh, and findeth them sleeping, and saith unto Peter, Simon, sleepest thou? couldest not thou watch one hour? 38 Watch ye and pray, lest ye enter into temptation. The spirit truly *is* ready, but the flesh *is* weak. 39 And again he went away, and prayed, and spake the same words. 40 And when he returned, he found them asleep again, (for their eyes were heavy,) neither wist they what to answer him. 41 And he cometh the third time, and saith unto them, Sleep on now, and take *your* rest: it is enough, the hour is come; behold, the Son of man is betrayed into the hands of sinners. 42 Rise up, let us go; lo, he that betray-eth me is at hand. 43 ¶ And immediately, while he yet spake, cometh Judas, one of the twelve, and with him a great multitude with swords and staves, from the chief priests and the scribes and the elders. 44 And he that betrayed him had given them a token, saying, Whomsoever I shall kiss, that same is he; take him, and lead *him* away safely. 45 And as soon as he was come, he goeth straightway to him, and saith, Master, Master; and kissed him. 46 ¶ And they laid their hands on him, and took him. 47 And one of them that stood by drew a sword, and smote a servant of the high priest, and cut off his ear. 48 And Jesus answered and said unto them, Are ye come out, as against a thief, with swords and *with* staves to take me? 49 I was daily with you in the temple teaching, and ye took me not: but the Scriptures must be fulfilled. 50 And they all forsook him, and fled. 51 And there followed him a certain young man, having a linen cloth cast about *his* naked *body;* and tne young men laid hold on him: 52 And he left the linen cloth, and fled from them naked. 53 ¶ And they led Jesus away to the high priest: and with him were assembled all the chief priests and the elders and the scribes. 54 And Peter followed him afar off, even into the palace of the high priest: and he sat with the servants, and warmed himself at the fire. 55 And the chief priests and all the council sought for witness against Jesus to put him to death; and found none. 56 For many bare false witness against him, but their witness agreed not together.

1 Or, *Watch ye, and pray that ye enter not*
2 Gr. *kissed him much.*
3 Gr. *bondservant.*

37 what thou wilt. And he cometh, and findeth them sleeping, and saith unto Peter, Simon, sleepest thou?
38 couldest thou not watch one hour? ¹ Watch and pray, that ye enter not into temptation: the spirit indeed is
39 willing, but the flesh is weak. And again he went
40 away, and prayed, saying the same words. And again he came, and found them sleeping, for their eyes were very heavy; and they knew not what to answer him.
41 And he cometh the third time, and saith unto them, Sleep on now, and take your rest: it is enough; the hour is come; behold, the Son of man is betrayed into
42 the hands of sinners. Arise, let us be going: behold, he that betrayeth me is at hand.
43 And straightway, while he yet spake, cometh Judas, one of the twelve, and with him a multitude with swords and staves, from the chief priests and the
44 scribes and the elders. Now he that betrayed him had given them a token, saying, Whomsoever I shall kiss,
45 that is he; take him, and lead him away safely. And when he was come, straightway he came to him, and
46 saith, Rabbi; and ² kissed him. And they laid hands
47 on him, and took him. But a certain one of them that stood by drew his sword, and smote the ³ servant
48 of the high priest, and struck off his ear. And Jesus answered and said unto them, Are ye come out, as against a robber, with swords and staves to seize me?
49 I was daily with you in the temple teaching, and ye took me not: but *this is done* that the scriptures might
50 be fulfilled. And they all left him, and fled.
51 And a certain young man followed with him, having a linen cloth cast about him, over *his* naked *body*:
52 and they lay hold on him; but he left the linen cloth, and fled naked.
53 And they led Jesus away to the high priest: and there come together with him all the chief priests and
54 the elders and the scribes. And Peter had followed him afar off, even within, into the court of the high priest; and he was sitting with the officers, and warm-
55 ing himself in the light *of the fire*. Now the chief priests and the whole council sought witness against
56 Jesus to put him to death; and found it not. For

¹ Or, *Watch ye, and pray that ye enter not*

² Gr. *kissed him much.*

³ Gr. *bondservant.*

Eng. Revision. S. MARK. K. James Vers.

bare false witness against him, and their witness agreed not together. And there stood up certain, and bare false witness against him, saying, We heard him say, I will destroy this [1] temple that is made with hands, and in three days I will build another made without hands. And not even so did their witness agree together. And the high priest stood up in the midst, and asked Jesus, saying, Answerest thou nothing? what is it which these witness against thee? But he held his peace, and answered nothing. Again the high priest asked him, and saith unto him, Art thou the Christ, the Son of the Blessed? And Jesus said, I am: and ye shall see the Son of man sitting at the right hand of power, and coming with the clouds of heaven. And the high priest rent his clothes, and saith, What further need have we of witnesses? Ye have heard the blasphemy: what think ye? And they all condemned him to be [2] worthy of death. And some began to spit on him, and to cover his face, and to buffet him, and to say unto him, Prophesy: and the officers received him with [3] blows of their hands. And as Peter was beneath in the court, there cometh one of the maids of the high priest; and seeing Peter warming himself, she looked upon him, and saith, Thou also wast with the Nazarene, *even* Jesus. But he denied, saying, [4] I neither know, nor understand what thou sayest: and he went out into the [5] porch; [6] and the cock crew. And the maid saw him, and began again to say to them that stood by, This is *one* of them. But he again denied it. And after a little while again they that stood by said to Peter, Of a truth thou art *one* of them; for thou art a Galilæan. But he began to curse, and to swear, I know not this man of whom ye speak. And straightway the second time the cock crew. And Peter called to mind the word, how that Jesus said unto him, Before the cock crow twice, thou shalt deny me thrice. [7] And when he thought thereon, he wept.

15 And straightway in the morning the chief priests with the elders and scribes, and the whole council, held a consultation, and bound Jesus. and carried him away, and delivered him up to Pilate.

---

1 Or, *sanctuary*
2 Gr. *liable to.*
3 Or, *strokes of rods*
4 Or, *I neither know, nor understand: thou, what sayest thou ?*
5 Gr. *forecourt.*
6 Many ancient authorities omit *and the cock crew.*
7 Or, *And he began to weep.*

---

57 And there arose certain, and bare false witness against him, saying, 58 We heard him say, I will destroy this temple that is made with hands, and within three days I will build another made without hands. 59 But neither so did their witness agree together. 60 And the high priest stood up in the midst, and asked Jesus, saying, Answerest thou nothing? what *is it which* these witness against thee? 61 But he held his peace, and answered nothing. Again the high priest asked him, and said unto him, Art thou the Christ, the Son of the Blessed? 62 And Jesus said, I am: and ye shall see the Son of man sitting on the right hand of power, and coming in the clouds of heaven. 63 Then the high priest rent his clothes, and saith, What need we any further witnesses? 64 Ye have heard the blasphemy: what think ye? And they all condemned him to be guilty of death. 65 And some began to spit on him, and to cover his face, and to buffet him, and to say unto him, Prophesy: and the servants did strike him with the palms of their hands. 66 ¶ And as Peter was beneath in the palace, there cometh one of the maids of the high priest: 67 And when she saw Peter warming himself, she looked upon him, and said, And thou also wast with Jesus of Nazareth. 68 But he denied, saying, I know not, neither understand I what thou sayest. And he went out into the porch; and the cock crew. 69 And a maid saw him again, and began to say to them that stood by, This is *one* of them. 70 And he denied it again. And a little after, they that stood by said again to Peter, Surely thou art *one* of them: for thou art a Galilean, and thy speech agreeth *thereto*. 71 But he began to curse and to swear, *saying*, I know not this man of whom ye speak. 72 And the second time the cock crew. And Peter called to mind the word that Jesus said unto him, Before the cock crow twice, thou shalt deny me thrice. And when he thought thereon, he wept.

CHAPTER XV.

AND straightway in the morning the chief priests held a consultation with the elders and scribes and the whole council, and bound Jesus, and carried *him* away, and delivered *him* to Pilate.

many bare false witness against him, and their witness
57 agreed not together. And there stood up certain, and
58 bare false witness against him, saying, We heard him
say, I will destroy this ¹temple that is made with
hands, and in three days I will build another made
59 without hands. And not even so did their witness
60 agree together. And the high priest stood up in the
midst, and asked Jesus, saying, Answerest thou no-
61 thing? what is it which these witness against thee? But
he held his peace, and answered nothing. Again the
high priest asked him, and saith unto him, Art thou
62 the Christ, the Son of the Blessed? And Jesus said,
I am: and ye shall see the Son of man sitting at the
right hand of power, and coming with the clouds of
63 heaven. And the high priest rent his clothes, and
64 saith, What further need have we of witnesses? Ye
have heard the blasphemy: what think ye? And
65 they all condemned him to be ²worthy of death. And
some began to spit on him, and to cover his face, and
to buffet him, and to say unto him, Prophesy: and the
officers received him with ³blows of their hands.
66 And as Peter was beneath in the court, there cometh
67 one of the maids of the high priest; and seeing Peter
warming himself, she looked upon him, and saith,
68 Thou also wast with the Nazarene, *even* Jesus. But
he denied, saying, ⁴I neither know, nor understand
what thou sayest: and he went out into the ⁵porch;
69 ⁶and the cock crew. And the maid saw him, and
began again to say to them that stood by This is *one*
70 of them. But he again denied it. And after a little
while again they that stood by said to Peter, Of a
truth thou art *one* of them; for thou art a Galilæan.
71 But he began to curse, and to swear, I know not this
72 man of whom ye speak. And straightway the second
time the cock crew. And Peter called to mind the
word, how that Jesus said unto him, Before the cock
crow twice, thou shalt deny me thrice. ⁷And when he
thought thereon, he wept.
15 And straightway in the morning the chief priests
with the elders and scribes, and the whole council,
held a consultation, and bound Jesus, and carried

¹ Or, *sanctuary*

² Gr. *liable to.*

³ Or, *strokes of rods*

⁴ Or, *I neither know, nor understand: thou, what sayest thou?*

⁵ Gr. *forecourt.*

⁶ Many ancient authorities omit *and the cock crew.*

⁷ Or, *And he began to weep.*

Eng. Revision. S. MARK. K. James Vers.

2 And Pilate asked him, Art thou the King of the Jews? And he answering
3 saith unto him, Thou sayest. And the chief priests accused him of many
4 things. And Pilate again asked him, saying, Answerest thou nothing? behold how many things they accuse
5 thee of. But Jesus no more answered anything; insomuch that Pilate marvelled.
6 Now at ¹ the feast he used to release unto them one prisoner, whom they
7 asked of him. And there was one called Barabbas, *lying* bound with them that had made insurrection, men who in the insurrection had committed mur-
8 der. And the multitude went up and began to ask him *to do* as he was wont
9 to do unto them. And Pilate answered them, saying, Will ye that I release unto
10 you the King of the Jews? For he perceived that for envy the chief priests
11 had delivered him up. But the chief priests stirred up the multitude, that he should rather release Barabbas unto
12 them. And Pilate again answered and said unto them, What then shall I do unto him whom ye call the King of the
13 Jews? And they cried out again, Cru-
14 cify him. And Pilate said unto them, Why, what evil hath he done? But they cried out exceedingly, Crucify him.
15 And Pilate, wishing to content the multitude, released unto them Barabbas, and delivered Jesus, when he had scourged him, to be crucified.
16 And the soldiers led him away within the court, which is the ² Prætorium; and they call together the whole ³ band.
17 And they clothe him with purple, and plaiting a crown of thorns, they put it
18 on him; and they began to salute him,
19 Hail, King of the Jews! And they smote his head with a reed, and did spit upon him, and bowing their knees
20 worshipped him. And when they had mocked him, they took off from him the purple, and put on him his garments. And they lead him out to crucify him.
21 And they ⁴ compel one passing by, Simon of Cyrene, coming from the country, the father of Alexander and Rufus, to go *with them*, that he might bear his
22 cross. And they bring him unto the place Golgotha, which is, being inter-

1 Or, *a feast*
2 Or, *palace*
3 Or, *cohort*
4 Gr. *impress.*

2 And Pilate asked him, Art thou the King of the Jews? And he answering said unto him, Thou sayest *it.*
3 And the chief priests accused him of many things: but he answered nothing.
4 And Pilate asked him again, saying, Answerest thou nothing? behold how many things they witness against thee.
5 But Jesus yet answered nothing; so that Pilate marvelled.
6 Now at *that* feast he released unto them one prisoner, whomsoever they desired.
7 And there was *one* named Barabbas, *which lay* bound with them that had made insurrection with him, who had committed murder in the insurrection.
8 And the multitude crying aloud began to desire *him to do* as he had ever done unto them.
9 But Pilate answered them, saying, Will ye that I release unto you the King of the Jews?
10 For he knew that the chief priests had delivered him for envy.
11 But the chief priests moved the people, that he should rather release Barabbas unto them.
12 And Pilate answered and said again unto them, What will ye then that I shall do *unto him* whom ye call the King of the Jews?
13 And they cried out again, Crucify him.
14 Then Pilate said unto them, Why, what evil hath he done? And they cried out the more exceedingly, Crucify him.
15 ¶ And so Pilate, willing to content the people, released Barabbas unto them, and delivered Jesus, when he had scourged *him,* to be crucified.
16 And the soldiers led him away into the hall, called Pretorium; and they call together the whole band.
17 And they clothed him with purple, and platted a crown of thorns, and put it about his *head,*
18 And began to salute him, Hail, King of the Jews!
19 And they smote him on the head with a reed, and did spit upon him, and bowing *their* knees worshipped him.
20 And when they had mocked him, they took off the purple from him, and put his own clothes on him, and led him out to crucify him.
21 And they compel one Simon a Cyrenian, who passed by, coming out of the country, the father of Alexander and Rufus, to bear his cross.
22 And they bring him unto the place Golgotha, which is, being interpreted, The place of a skull.

2 him away, and delivered him up to Pilate. And Pilate asked him, Art thou the King of the Jews? And he
3 answering saith unto him, Thou sayest. And the chief
4 priests accused him of many things. And Pilate again asked him, saying, Answerest thou nothing? behold
5 how many things they accuse thee of. But Jesus no more answered anything; insomuch that Pilate marvelled.
6 Now at ¹the feast he used to release unto them one
7 prisoner, whom they asked of him. And there was one called Barabbas, *lying* bound with them that had made insurrection, men who in the insurrection had
8 committed murder. And the multitude went up and began to ask him *to do* as he was wont to do unto
9 them. And Pilate answered them, saying, Will ye
10 that I release unto you the King of the Jews? For he perceived that for envy the chief priests had de-
11 livered him up. But the chief priests stirred up the multitude, that he should rather release Barabbas unto
12 them. And Pilate again answered and said unto them, What then shall I do unto him whom ye call
13 the King of the Jews? And they cried out again,
14 Crucify him. And Pilate said unto them, Why, what evil hath he done? But they cried out exceedingly,
15 Crucify him. And Pilate, wishing to content the multitude, released unto them Barabbas, and delivered Jesus, when he had scourged him, to be crucified.
16 And the soldiers led him away within the court, which is the ²Prætorium; and they call together the
17 whole ³band. And they clothe him with purple, and
18 plaiting a crown of thorns, they put it on him; and they began to salute him, Hail, King of the Jews!
19 And they smote his head with a reed, and did spit upon him, and bowing their knees worshipped him.
20 And when they had mocked him, they took off from him the purple, and put on him his garments. And they lead him out to crucify him.
21 And they ⁴compel one passing by, Simon of Cyrene, coming from the country, the father of Alexander and Rufus, to go *with them*, that he might bear his cross.
22 And they bring him unto the place Golgotha, which

¹ Or, *a feast*

² Or, *palace*
³ Or, *cohort*

⁴ Gr. *impress*

Eng. Revision

23 preted, The place of a skull. And they offered him wine mingled with myrrh:
24 but he received it not. And they crucify him, and part his garments among them, casting lots upon them, what
25 each should take. And it was the third
26 hour, and they crucified him. And the superscription of his accusation was written over, THE KING OF THE JEWS.
27 And with him they crucify two robbers; one on his right hand, and one on
29 his left.[1] And they that passed by railed on him, wagging their heads, and saying, Ha! thou that destroyest the [2]temple, and buildest it in three
30 days, save thyself, and come down from
31 the cross. In like manner also the chief priests mocking *him* among themselves with the scribes said, He saved others;
32 [3]himself he cannot save. Let the Christ, the King of Israel, now come down from the cross, that we may see and believe. And they that were crucified with him reproached him.
33 And when the sixth hour was come, there was darkness over the whole
34 [4]land until the ninth hour. And at the ninth hour Jesus cried with a loud voice, Eloi, Eloi, lama sabachthani? which is, being interpreted, My God, my God,
35 [5]why hast thou forsaken me? And some of them that stood by, when they heard it, said, Behold, he calleth Elijah.
36 And one ran, and filling a sponge full of vinegar, put it on a reed, and gave him to drink, saying, Let be; let us see whether Elijah cometh to take him
37 down. And Jesus uttered a loud voice,
38 and gave up the ghost. And the veil of the [7]temple was rent in twain from the
39 top to the bottom. And when the centurion, which stood by over against him, saw that he [6]so gave up the ghost, he said, Truly this man was [7]the Son of
40 God. And there were also women beholding from afar: among whom *were* both Mary Magdalene, and Mary the mother of James the [8]less and of Joses,
41 and Salome; who, when he was in Galilee, followed him, and ministered unto him; and many other women which came up with him unto Jerusalem.
42 And when even was now come, because it was the Preparation, that is,
43 the day before the sabbath, there came

---

1 Many ancient authorities insert ver. 28 *And the scripture was fulfilled, which saith, And he was reckoned with transgressors.* See Luke xxii. 37.
2 Or, *sanctuary*
3 Or, *can he not save himself?*
4 Or, *earth*
5 Or, *why didst thou forsake me?*
6 Many ancient authorities read *so cried out, and gave up the ghost.*
7 Or, *a son of God*
8 Gr. *little.*

K. James Vers.

23 And they gave him to drink wine mingled with myrrh: but he received *it* not.
24 And when they had crucified him, they parted his garments, casting lots upon them, what every man should take.
25 And it was the third hour, and they crucified him.
26 And the superscription of his accusation was written over, THE KING OF THE JEWS.
27 And with him they crucify two thieves; the one on his right hand, and the other on his left.
28 And the Scripture was fulfilled, which saith, And he was numbered with the transgressors.
29 And they that passed by railed on him, wagging their heads, and saying, Ah, thou that destroyest the temple, and buildest *it* in three days,
30 Save thyself, and come down from the cross.
31 Likewise also the chief priests mocking said among themselves with the scribes, He saved others; himself he cannot save.
32 Let Christ the King of Israel descend now from the cross, that we may see and believe. And they that were crucified with him reviled him.
33 And when the sixth hour was come, there was darkness over the whole land until the ninth hour.
34 And at the ninth hour Jesus cried with a loud voice, saying, Eloi, Eloi, lama sabachthani? which is, being interpreted, My God, my God, why hast thou forsaken me?
35 And some of them that stood by, when they heard *it*, said, Behold, he calleth Elias.
36 And one ran and filled a sponge full of vinegar, and put *it* on a reed, and gave him to drink, saying, Let alone: let us see whether Elias will come to take him down.
37 And Jesus cried with a loud voice, and gave up the ghost.
38 And the vail of the temple was rent in twain from the top to the bottom.
39 ¶ And when the centurion, which stood over against him, saw that he so cried out, and gave up the ghost, he said, Truly this man was the Son of God.
40 There were also women looking on afar off: among whom was Mary Magdalene, and Mary the mother of James the less and of Joses, and Salome;
41 Who also, when he was in Galilee, followed him, and ministered unto him; and many other women which came up with him unto Jerusalem.
42 ¶ And now when the even was come, because it was the preparation, that is, the day before the sabbath,

23 is, being interpreted, The place of a skull. And they offered him wine mingled with myrrh: but he received
24 it not. And they crucify him, and part his garments among them, casting lots upon them, what each should
25 take. And it was the third hour, and they crucified
26 him. And the superscription of his accusation was writ-
27 ten over, THE KING OF THE JEWS. And with him they crucify two robbers; one on his right hand, and one
29 on his left.¹ And they that passed by railed on him, wagging their heads, and saying, Ha! thou that destroyest the ²temple, and buildest it in three days,
30 save thyself, and come down from the cross. In like
31 manner also the chief priests mocking *him* among themselves with the scribes said, He saved others;
32 ³himself he cannot save. Let the Christ, the King of Israel, now come down from the cross, that we may see and believe. And they that were crucified with him reproached him.
33 And when the sixth hour was come, there was darkness over the whole ⁴land until the ninth hour.
34 And at the ninth hour Jesus cried with a loud voice, Eloi, Eloi, lama sabachthani? which is, being interpreted, My God, my God, ⁵why hast thou forsaken
35 me? And some of them that stood by, when they
36 heard it, said, Behold, he calleth Elijah. And one ran, and filling a sponge full of vinegar, put it on a reed, and gave him to drink, saying, Let be; let us
37 see whether Elijah cometh to take him down. And Jesus uttered a loud voice, and gave up the ghost.
38 And the veil of the ²temple was rent in twain from
39 the top to the bottom. And when the centurion, who stood by over against him, saw that he ⁶so gave up the ghost, he said, Truly this man was ⁷the Son of
40 God. And there were also women beholding from afar: among whom *were* both Mary Magdalene, and Mary the mother of James the ⁸less and of Joses,
41 and Salome; who, when he was in Galilee, followed him, and ministered unto him; and many other women that came up with him unto Jerusalem.
42 And when even was now come, because it was the
43 Preparation, that is, the day before the sabbath, there

¹ Many ancient authorities insert ver. 28 *And the scripture was fulfilled, which saith, And he was reckoned with transgressors.* See Luke xxii. 37.
² Or, *sanctuary*
³ Or, *can he not save himself?*
⁴ Or, *earth*
⁵ Or, *why didst thou forsake me?*
⁶ Many ancient authorities read *so cried out, and gave up the ghost.*
⁷ Or, *a son of God*
⁸ Gr. *little.*

Eng. Revision.	K. James Vers.
Joseph of Arimathæa, a councillor of honourable estate, who also himself was looking for the kingdom of God; and he boldly went in unto Pilate, and 44 asked for the body of Jesus. And Pilate marvelled if he were already dead: and calling unto him the centurion, he asked him whether he ¹ had been any 45 while dead. And when he learned it of the centurion, he granted the corpse to 46 Joseph. And he bought a linen cloth, and taking him down, wound him in the linen cloth, and laid him in a tomb which had been hewn out of a rock; and he rolled a stone against the door 47 of the tomb. And Mary Magdalene and Mary the *mother* of Joses beheld where he was laid.	43 Joseph of Arimathea, an honourable counsellor, which also waited for the kingdom of God, came, and went in boldly unto Pilate, and craved the body of Jesus. 44 And Pilate marvelled if he were already dead: and calling *unto him* the centurion, he asked him whether he had been any while dead. 45 And when he knew *it* of the centurion, he gave the body to Joseph. 46 And he bought fine linen, and took him down, and wrapped him in the linen, and laid him in a sepulchre which was hewn out of a rock, and rolled a stone unto the door of the sepulchre. 47 And Mary Magdalene and Mary *the mother* of Joses beheld where he was laid.
16 And when the sabbath was past, Mary Magdalene, and Mary the *mother* of James, and Salome, bought spices, that they might come and anoint him. 2 And very early on the first day of the week, they come to the tomb when the 3 sun was risen. And they were saying among themselves, Who shall roll us away the stone from the door of the 4 tomb? and looking up, they see that the stone is rolled back: for it was ex-5 ceeding great. And entering into the tomb, they saw a young man sitting on the right side, arrayed in a white robe; 6 and they were amazed. And he saith unto them, Be not amazed: ye seek Jesus, the Nazarene, which hath been crucified: he is risen; he is not here: behold, the place where they laid him! 7 But go, tell his disciples and Peter, He goeth before you into Galilee: there shall ye see him, as he said unto you. 8 And they went out, and fled from the tomb; for trembling and astonishment had come upon them: and they said nothing to any one; for they were afraid.	CHAPTER XVI. AND when the sabbath was past, Mary Magdalene, and Mary the *mother* of James, and Salome, had bought sweet spices, that they might come and anoint him. 2 And very early in the morning, the first *day* of the week, they came unto the sepulchre at the rising of the sun. 3 And they said among themselves, Who shall roll us away the stone from the door of the sepulchre? 4 And when they looked, they saw that the stone was rolled away: for it was very great. 5 And entering into the sepulchre, they saw a young man sitting on the right side, clothed in a long white garment; and they were affrighted. 6 And he saith unto them, Be not affrighted: ye seek Jesus of Nazareth, which was crucified: he is risen; he is not here: behold the place where they laid him. 7 But go your way, tell his disciples and Peter that he goeth before you into Galilee: there shall ye see him, as he said unto you. 8 And they went out quickly, and fled from the sepulchre; for they trembled and were amazed: neither said they any thing to any *man;* for they were afraid.
9 ² Now when he was risen early on the first day of the week, he appeared first to Mary Magdalene, from whom he had 10 cast out seven ³ devils. She went and told them that had been with him, as	9 ¶ Now when *Jesus* was risen early the first *day* of the week, he appeared first to Mary Magdalene, out of whom he had cast seven devils. 10 *And* she went and told them that had been with him, as they mourned and wept.

1 Many ancient authorities read *were already dead.*
2 The two oldest Greek manuscripts, and some other authorities, omit from ver. 9 to the end. Some other authorities have a different ending to the Gospel.
3 Gr. *demons.*

came Joseph of Arimathæa, a councillor of honourable estate, who also himself was looking for the kingdom of God; and he boldly went in unto Pilate, and asked for the body of Jesus. And Pilate marvelled if he were already dead: and calling unto him the centurion, he asked him whether he [1]had been any while dead. And when he learned it of the centurion, he granted the corpse to Joseph. And he bought a linen cloth, and taking him down, wound him in the linen cloth, and laid him in a tomb which had been hewn out of a rock; and he rolled a stone against the door of the tomb. And Mary Magdalene and Mary the *mother* of Joses beheld where he was laid.

16 And when the sabbath was past, Mary Magdalene, and Mary the *mother* of James, and Salome, bought spices, that they might come and anoint him. And very early on the first day of the week, they come to the tomb when the sun was risen. And they were saying among themselves, Who shall roll us away the stone from the door of the tomb? and looking up, they see that the stone is rolled back: for it was exceeding great. And entering into the tomb, they saw a young man sitting on the right side, arrayed in a white robe; and they were amazed. And he saith unto them, Be not amazed: ye seek Jesus, the Nazarene, who hath been crucified: he is risen; he is not here: behold, the place where they laid him! But go, tell his disciples and Peter, He goeth before you into Galilee: there shall ye see him, as he said unto you. And they went out, and fled from the tomb; for trembling and astonishment had come upon them: and they said nothing to any one; for they were afraid.

9 [2]Now when he was risen early on the first day of the week, he appeared first to Mary Magdalene, from whom he had cast out seven demons. She went and told them that had been with him, as they mourned

[1] Many ancient authorities read *were already dead*.

[2] The two oldest Greek manuscripts, and some other authorities, omit from ver. 9 to the end. Some other authorities have a different ending to the Gospel.

11 they mourned and wept. And they, when they heard that he was alive, and had been seen of her, disbelieved.
12 And after these things he was manifested in another form unto two of them, as they walked, on their way
13 into the country. And they went away and told it unto the rest: neither believed they them.
14 And afterward he was manifested unto the eleven themselves as they sat at meat; and he upbraided them with their unbelief and hardness of heart, because they believed not them which
15 had seen him after he was risen. And he said unto them, Go ye into all the world, and preach the gospel to the
16 whole creation. He that believeth and is baptized shall be saved; but he that
17 disbelieveth shall be condemned. And these signs shall follow them that believe: in my name shall they cast out [1] devils; they shall speak with [2] new
18 tongues; they shall take up serpents, and if they drink any deadly thing, it shall in no wise hurt them; they shall lay hands on the sick, and they shall recover.
19 So then the Lord Jesus, after he had spoken unto them, was received up into heaven, and sat down at the right hand
20 of God. And they went forth, and preached everywhere, the Lord working with them, and confirming the word by the signs that followed. Amen.

1 Gr. *demons.*
2 Some ancient authorities omit *new.*

11 And they, when they had heard that he was alive, and had been seen of her, believed not.
12 ¶ After that he appeared in another form unto two of them, as they walked, and went into the country.
13 And they went and told *it* unto the residue: neither believed they them.
14 ¶ Afterward he appeared unto the eleven as they sat at meat, and upbraided them with their unbelief and hardness of heart, because they believed not them which had seen him after he was risen.
15 And he said unto them, Go ye into all the world, and preach the gospel to every creature.
16 He that believeth and is baptized shall be saved; but he that believeth not shall be damned.
17 And these signs shall follow them that believe; In my name shall they cast out devils; they shall speak with new tongues;
18 They shall take up serpents; and if they drink any deadly thing, it shall not hurt them; they shall lay hands on the sick, and they shall recover.
19 ¶ So then, after the Lord had spoken unto them, he was received up into heaven, and sat on the right hand of God.
20 And they went forth, and preached every where, the Lord working with *them*, and confirming the word with signs following. Amen.

11 and wept. And they, when they heard that he was alive, and had been seen of her, disbelieved.
12 And after these things he was manifested in another form unto two of them, as they walked, on their
13 way into the country. And they went away and told it unto the rest: neither believed they them.
14 And afterward he was manifested unto the eleven themselves as they sat at meat; and he upbraided them with their unbelief and hardness of heart, because they believed not them who had seen him
15 after he was risen. And he said unto them, Go ye into all the world, and preach the gospel to the whole
16 creation. He that believeth and is baptized shall be saved; but he that disbelieveth shall be condemned.
17 And these signs shall follow them that believe: in my name shall they cast out demons; they shall speak
18 with ¹ new tongues; they shall take up serpents, and if they drink any deadly thing, it shall in no wise hurt them; they shall lay hands on the sick, and they shall recover.
19 So then the Lord Jesus, after he had spoken unto them, was received up into heaven, and sat down at
20 the right hand of God. And they went forth, and preached everywhere, the Lord working with them, and confirming the word by the signs that followed. Amen.

¹ Some ancient authorities omit *new*.

OF

EVENTS IN THE LIFE OF CHRIST; WITH PAGE REFERENCES TO THOSE MENTIONED IN MARK'S GOSPEL.

[*From "The Gospel History," by* Rev. LYMAN ABBOTT, D.D., *and* J. R. GILMORE.]

			PAGE
An angel appears to Zacharias...............	2	B.C.	
An angel appears to Mary...................	1	"	
Mary visits Elizabeth.......................	1	"	
Birth of John the Baptist...................	1	"	
Birth of Jesus.............................	1	J.C.	
The circumcision of Jesus..................	1	"	
The visit of the Magi......................	1	"	
The flight into Egypt......................	1	"	
The return from Egypt.....................		"	
Jesus goes with his parents to the Passover..	12	"	
Preaching of John the Baptist...............	30	"	62
The baptism of Jesus......................	31	"	62
The temptation of Jesus...................	31	"	62
Testimony of John the Baptist to Jesus......Jan.-Feb.,	31	"	62
The first disciples.........................Jan.-Feb.,	31	"	63
The marriage at Cana of Galilee............Jan.-Feb.,	31	"	
Jesus drives the traders from the temple.....April 11-18,	31	"	
Jesus discourses with Nicodemus...........April 11-18,	31	"	
The first Judean ministry..................April-Dec.,	31	"	
Jesus departs to Galilee...................April-Dec.,	31	"	
Jesus talks with the Samaritan woman......April-Dec.,	31	"	
At Cana heals the nobleman's servant of Capernaum.April-Dec.,	31	"	
Heals the impotent man at Jerusalem......Mar. 30-April 5,	32	"	
John the Baptist cast into prison..........Mar. 30-April 5,	32	"	62, 73
Jesus goes again to Galilee and begins to preach publicly...............................	April,	32	"	
Rejected at Nazareth......................	April,	32	"	72
Makes His residence at Capernaum.........	April,	32	"	
The call of Simon and Andrew, James and John, with the miraculous draught of fishes........March-April,	32	"	63
Healing of a demoniac in synagogue.........March-April,	32	"	63
Healing of Peter's wife's mother...........March-April,	32	"	63
A circuit throughout Galilee...............March-April,	32	"	64
Healing of a leper........................Summer,	32	"	64
Healing of a paralytic at Capernaum.......Summer,	32	"	64
The call of Matthew......................Summer,	32	"	65
The disciples pluck the ears of corn.........Summer,	32	"	66
The healing of the withered hand...........Summer,	32	"	66
A call of the Twelve Apostles..............Summer,	32	"	67
The Sermon on the Mount.................Summer,	32	"	
Heals the centurion's servant...............Summer,	32	"	
The raising of the widow's son.............Summer,	32	"	
John in prison sends disciples to Jesus.......Summer,	32	"	
Jesus anointed by a woman who was a sinner...Summer,	32	"	
A second circuit in Galilee.................Autumn,	32	"	67
Blasphemy against the Holy Ghost..........			67
Interruption of his Mother and Brethren.....			68
Parables: The Sower; Mustard Seed; Candle.....			68, 69
Heals blind and dumb demoniac............Autumn,	32	"	
The Pharisees seek a sign..................Autumn,	32	"	78
Jesus teaches in parables...................Autumn,	32	"	68
Jesus visits Decapolis......................Autumn,	32	"	70

CHRONOLOGICAL INDEX.

			PAGE
Stills the tempest...	Autumn, 32	J.C.	70
Heals a demoniac at Gadara...	Autumn, 32	"	70
Levi's feast. ...	Autumn, 32	"	
The raising of the daughter of Jairus...	Autumn, 32	"	71
The healing of an infirm woman...	Autumn, 32	"	71
Two blind men healed...	Autumn, 32	"	
Second visit to Nazareth...	Winter, 33	"	72
Sending of the Twelve...	Winter, 33	"	73
Death of Baptist; Jesus returns to Capernaum...	Winter, 33	"	73
Crossing of the sea, and feeding of the 5000; return to Capernaum	Spring, 33	"	75
Discourse at Capernaum...	April, 33	"	76
Jesus visits the coasts of Tyre and Sidon; heals the daughter of Syro-Phœnician woman; visits the region of Decapolis; heals one with an impediment in his speech; feeds the 4000...	Summer, 33	"	77, 78
Jesus returns to Capernaum; is tempted by the Pharisees; reproves their hypocrisy; again crosses the sea; heals blind man at Bethsaida...	Summer, 33	"	78, 79
Peter's confession that He is the Christ; He announces His approaching death and resurrection.	Summer, 33	"	79, 82
The transfiguration. ...	Summer, 33	"	80
Healing of lunatic child...	Summer, 33	"	81
Jesus journeys through Galilee, teaching the disciples...	Autumn, 33	"	82
Goes up to Feast of Tabernacles...	Autumn, 33	"	
He teaches in the temple; efforts to arrest him...	Oct., 33	"	
An adulteress is brought before him; attempt to stone Him...	Oct., 33	"	
Healing of a man blind from birth; return to Galilee...	Oct., 33	"	
Final departure from Galilee; is rejected at Samaria; sending of the Seventy, whom He follows...	Nov., 33	"	
Jesus is attended by great multitudes; parable of the good Samaritan...	Nov., 33	"	
Dining with a Pharisee...	Nov.-Dec., 33	"	
Jesus rebukes hypocrisy...	Nov.-Dec., 33	"	
Parable of the rich fool...	Nov.-Dec., 33	"	
Jesus is told of the murder of the Galileans by Pilate; parable of the fig-tree; healing of a woman 18 years sick; is warned against Herod.	Nov.-Dec., 33	"	
Feast of Dedication; visit to Mary and Martha; the Jews at Jerusalem attempt to stone Him; He goes beyond Jordan...	Dec., 33	"	
Jesus dines with a Pharisee, and heals a man with dropsy; parables of the great supper, of the lost sheep, of the lost piece of silver, of the unjust steward, of the rich man and Lazarus...	Dec., 33	"	
Resurrection of Lazarus; counsel of the Jews to put Him to death; He retires to Ephraim...	Jan.-Feb., 34	"	
Sojourn in Ephraim till Passover at hand; journeys on the border of Samaria and Galilee; healing of ten lepers; parables of the unjust judge, and of Pharisee and publican...	Feb.-March, 34	"	
Teaching respecting divorce; blessing of children; the young ruler...	Feb.-March, 34	"	83, 84
Parable of laborers in the vineyard...			
Jesus again announces His death; ambition of James and John...	March, 34	"	85
Blind men at Jericho; departure to Bethany...	March, 34	"	85
Zaccheus; parable of the pounds...			
Supper at Bethany, and anointing of Jesus by Mary.	Sat., March, 31, 34	"	93

CHRONOLOGICAL INDEX.

			PAGE
Entry into Jerusalem; visit to the temple, and return to Bethany................................Sund., April 1, 34	J.C.	86
Cursing of the fig-tree; second purification of the temple; return to Bethany................Mond., April 1, 34	"	86
Teaching in the temple; parable of the two sons, of the wicked husbandmen, of the king's son; attempts of His enemies to entangle Him; the poor widow; the Greeks who desire to see Him; a voice heard from heaven; departure from the temple to the Mount of Olives; discourse respecting the end of the world; return to Bethany; agreement of Judas with the priests to betray Him...Tues., April 3, 34	"	88–93
Jesus seeks retirement at Bethany...............Wed., April 4, 34	"	
Sending of Peter and John to prepare the Passover; the paschal supper........................Thurs., April 5, 34	"	93, 94
Events at paschal supper..................Thurs. eve., April 5, 34	"	94
After supper Jesus foretells the denials of Peter; speaks of the coming of the Comforter, and ends with prayer............................Thurs. eve., April 5, 34	"	94
Jesus in the garden of Gethsemane........Thurs. eve., April 5, 34	"	94
Betrayed by Judas.................................		95
Jesus is led to the house of Annas, and thence to the palace of Caiaphas; is condemned for blasphemy..................................Friday, 1–5 A.M., April 6, 34	"	95
Peter's denial..		96
Taken before Pilate...............Friday, 5–6 A.M., April 6, 34	"	97
Charge of sedition; Pilate finds no fault with Him, and attempts to release Him, but is forced to scourge Him, and give Him up to be crucified. Friday, 6–9 A.M., April 6, 34	"	97
Jesus is crucified at Golgotha.......Friday, 9–12 A.M., April 6, 34	"	98
Upon the cross is reviled by His enemies; commends His mother to John; darkness covers the land; He dies; the earth shakes, and rocks are rent. Friday, 12 A.M.–3 P.M., April 6, 34	"	98
His body taken down and given to Joseph, and laid in his sepulchre...................Friday, 3–6 P.M., April 6, 34	"	99
Resurrection of Jesus, and appearance to Mary Magdalene......... ....Sunday, A.M., April 8, 34	"	99
Appearance to the two disciples at Emmaus; to Peter and to the Eleven at Jerusalem. Sunday, P.M., April 8, 34	"	100
Appearance to the apostles and Thomas.....Sunday, April 15, 34	"	100
Appearance to seven disciples at sea of Tiberias, and to 500 at mountain in Galilee................April–May, 34	"	
Final appearance to the disciples at Jerusalem, and ascension to heaven....................Thursday, May 18, 34	"	100

www.ingramcontent.com/pod-product-compliance
Lightning Source LLC
Chambersburg PA
CBHW020302090426
42735CB00009B/1186